LABOUR IN CANADA

DESMOND MORTON

Grolier Limited
TORONTO

FOCUS ON CANADIAN HISTORY SERIES

SERIES CONSULTANT: DESMOND MORTON

Dedicated to Jim Bury, who taught me that the
fundamental of unionism was humanity.

*Cover: Winnipeg, June 21, 1919. A crowd gathers to protest the arrest of the
leaders of the Winnipeg General Strike.*

Cover design: Cheryl Trevers

Illustration credits: Public Archives of Canada, cover (C 18864) and pages 31
(C 43179), 32 (WS 66), 34 (PA 8405), 42 (C 28574), 48 (WS 1650), 61 (PA 35676),
66 (PA 115252), 71 (C 53646), 73 (PA 80753), 75 (Weekend Magazine Collection);
United Steelworkers, pages 9, 15, 39, 81; Canadian Paperworkers Union, pages 12,
85; Labour Gazette, pages 16, 25, 82; Canadian Union of Public Employees, pages 19,
88; Vivien Brody, page 28; Ontario Archives, page 45; Manitoba Archives, pages 49,
58; David Lewis, page 52; Archives of Labor and Urban Affairs, Wayne State University, pages 62, 72; New Democratic Party, page 77; Julien Labourdais, page 86.

Canadian Cataloguing in Publication Data

Morton, Desmond, 1937-
   Labour in Canada

(Focus on Canadian history series)
Includes index.
ISBN 0-7172-1820-1

1. Trade-unions—Canada—History.
2. Labour and labouring classes—Canada—History.
I. Title.

HD6524.M67   331.88′0971   C82-094450-5

1234567890   AP   098765432

Printed and Bound in Canada

Contents

Introduction

Most of Canadian history seems to be written about governors and prime ministers and other powerful people. Yet when we look at our country, we see that most of the work has been done by people whose names we never hear. They built the canals and the railways. They put up the great buildings and our own homes. They produce the food we eat and the things we use.

This is a book about these people—the ordinary workers. It is also about how the lives of workers have improved in the last century or more. Mainly, it is a book about the people and organizations which brought about those changes. It is a book about unions, governments and individual men and women who were not content to leave things as they always had been.

Almost everyone works for a living—or would like to. Unfortunately, a complicated "industrialized" society has forced more and more people to obey orders in their work. Skilled craftsmen became factory workers. Men and women who could make shoes from a piece of raw leather had to learn to tend a machine that stamped out a heel or a sole. They lost forever the personal freedom and self-respect they had had as craftsmen. However, they found that they could win back some power and respect by forming unions.

More and more working people have united to win better treatment and more respect. Forty years ago, laws began to change so that millions of Canadians who had never had the chance to join unions could do so. More recently, professional people like nurses, teachers and engineers have formed unions. Like the skilled craft workers of a century ago, these professionals have felt that they are losing their freedom as individuals.

Of course, not all Canadians choose unions. Many people still choose to take the risks of being a farmer or a small business operator because their personal freedom is worth the price. Other people have positions that are deeply satisfying, despite extra work and responsibility. Many Canadian workers who might join unions prefer not to do so for personal or religious reasons. Others feel no need to join—in part because all workers in Canada benefit from union influences on wages and conditions.

This book has been written to tell you more than the history of unions in Canada. It also tries to explain how and why unions operate as they do. Through unions, workers and their employers have brought a kind of economic democracy to the workplace. For all the problems and imperfections, it is a great achievement. We have all shared in the benefits.

Local 357 and Other Unions

It was almost 8 P.M. when Ann reached the drab cement-block building on 14th Street. She felt nervous as she went down the stairs to the basement. After working five months at Gamble's, this was her first union meeting. She had had to join the union, but that didn't mean that she had to give up her free time.

Ann peered through the haze of cigarette smoke, hunting for a friendly face. Then she saw Maria Moretti beckoning to her. It was Maria, the union shop steward in her department, who had urged her to come. Now Maria lifted her huge black handbag from an adjoining seat as Ann squeezed down the row of battered folding chairs.

"Good to see you, kid. Been saving a seat for you," Maria greeted her. "You've met Sylvia Emerson, haven't you? And this is Al Montgomery. He was at Labour College last summer. Bet he's bucking for a union staff job." A young black man smiled at her.

"No way, Maria. One summer away taught me that I like my family too much."

At the front of the hall, the buzz of talk died away. Men and women filed into a row of chairs on a platform under a huge plaster replica of the union badge. A big, balding man stood, nodded to a few friends in the audience and spoke in a voice that needed no help from a microphone.

"Brothers and Sisters, this special meeting of Local 357 will now come to order. I'm glad to see so many of you could make it tonight. We're here because negotiations are at a pretty critical stage for your bargaining committee. For that reason, I'll ask the guard to tile the doors."

"It's okay", Maria whispered. "That's just an old union term for making this a secret meeting. Foghorn Sweeney"—she gestured at the

president—"doesn't want anyone telling the company what we decide."

Next, a thin, angular woman was reading the minutes of the previous meeting at such a pace that Ann could hardly follow her.

Maria leaned over. "That's Marg Wilmoff from Accounting. If you really want to know what happened at a meeting, you read it in the union paper. But Marg's a marvel for getting the details right."

As the secretary sat down, the union president was on his feet.

"Our main business is a report from our negotiating committee." He glanced behind him. "Bill Scranton, the chairman, is here now, but first I'd like to introduce someone who has been giving us a whole lot of help. Sister Helen Toyama is an economist at union headquarters and she's been sitting in on our negotiations. Maybe she'd like to say a few words."

A young woman climbed to the stage and walked to a microphone.

"I hope you don't mind me using this thing", she smiled, but not many of us have a voice like your president. I bet Old Man Gamble can hear him all the way out to the cemetery." There was laughter. "I think that Gamble Industries is getting the message from the union, too. Once we showed that we had a case and a good grasp of their profits for the past three years, they moved a long way from their first offer. If we stick together and use our heads, I predict that you'll get the best contract in the industry."

Bill Scranton was next. Ann recognized him as her kid brother's hockey coach.

"Helen gave you the good news," Scranton started, "I've got the bad. Helen is right. With her help, the company has moved a long way from its first position, but we're not going to get everything we asked for either. Remember that two of the things we wanted in this new contract were early retirement and paid maternity leave."

"Yeah, and we'll strike if we don't get them both," shouted a young man a few seats in front of Ann. A few cheers echoed the outburst.

"The brother says he wants them both," Scranton continued, "and so does your negotiating committee, but we won't get them without a long strike. No company in our industry has the kind of contract we want. I believe—and Helen and the rest of the committee agree with me—that we can win the maternity leave or early retirement and still get a settlement without a strike. But don't kid yourself. With the

Union and management meet across the bargaining table to settle a contract between the Potash Corporation of Saskatchewan and the United Steelworkers. About 95 percent of all contracts are settled without strikes or lockouts.

state of the market, any strike this year will be a long one. That's why I move, seconded by your committee, that we go for the maternity leave.''

At once, the hall buzzed with whispers. Ann sensed the anger at Scranton's words. After a few words from Maria, Sylvia Emerson got up and made her way to a microphone in the aisle. Others had already gathered there for a chance to speak.

''Now you'll see the fireworks'', Maria whispered into Ann's ear. ''A lot of the members want the early retirement, but our union voted last year that maternity leave would be its top priority. And we've just got to win. Right now, a woman has to quit and go on unemployment insurance when she's going to have a baby. With inflation and the cost of everything, that's a disaster. But if we had a strike, a lot of people here could lose their homes. . . .''

Ann looked around at her fellow union members, trying to read their minds. She remembered how her mom and dad had gone short when the younger children had come along.

By now, two more people had spoken. An older man had called on the union to fight for early retirement. His speech, emotional and personal, had drawn cheers and applause. There was support, too, for a woman of Ann's age who had demanded to know if Local 357 had lost the courage to fight for its members. Then there were more speakers for the early retirement clause. One of them recalled that the union had also dropped the demand during negotiations two years before. Now it was Sylvia Emerson's turn.

"Brothers and Sisters", she began, her voice hoarse and nervous, "we made up our minds two years ago to go for maternity leave and it was dropped, too. This is something our whole union backed at the last convention. And look, it isn't something just for women. Men have families too. My husband and I have had two children and we both know what it's like to go on the pogey when you have to meet payments. With kids, you need more money, not less, and that's true whether you're a wife or a husband."

Flushed and breathing heavily, Sylvia threaded her way back to her seat.

"Hey Maria," she gasped, "I never thought I could do it."

"You were great", Maria grinned and reached out to hug her.

The debate droned on but few speakers echoed Sylvia's appeal. Now, Ann noticed, Maria looked worried. And even Ann had second thoughts. Maybe it was selfish to ask for maternity leave. She knew that her own dad longed to retire from the boring, dirty job that left him just a little more tired each weekend. By now, there was a din of conversation in the hall. Twice the president had rapped his gavel and roared out a demand for order. Suddenly, the hall grew silent. At the microphone stood a stubby, grizzled man in a shabby tweed suit.

"Hey, that's Jack McLeod". Maria almost giggled with pleasure. "He'll give them a speech."

McLeod started in a low voice, compelling people to listen. Then his voice rose, the faint Scottish accent growing stronger.

"Some of you know me," McLeod began, "and many of you don't. I was here when we started Local 357 back in 1937, when some of your dads earned forty-one cents an hour and your moms earned twenty-five cents if they were lucky. I was the second fellow that old man Gamble fired for trying to start a union. But I outlived him, and when I came back from the war, we got the union. I went through the 1946 strike and the 1963 strike. If anyone deserves early retirement, I do, and I'd be out the factory gate before any of you if the clause goes through."

Now there were cheers and whistles.

"But," roared McLeod, "we aren't going after early retirement this year because our union doesn't exist for people who just think about themselves. And we're not going to have a strike. This local union is too smart to ruin its members and this company in a fight we can't win."

Now there were no cheers and Ann could feel the tension.

"Brothers and Sisters," McLeod's voice was soft now and the hall was absolutely silent, "we've heard all the arguments for and against paid maternity leave. Some say it's a new idea. Some say it's just for women. Let me remind you of two things. First, unions exist to fight for impossible new ideas—like paid vacations and the forty-hour week it took us until 1964 to win. Second, there is no such thing as a benefit just for men or for women or for the old or the young. Local 357 is a union for all of us. Tonight, we will keep faith with this union. I'm backing Brother Scranton's committee."

As McLeod walked stiffly back to his seat, applause burst from the audience. There were shouts of "Vote!" The president banged his gavel.

"Are you ready for the vote?" There were some protests and more shouts of agreement. Another bang on the gavel. "All in favour of the maternity leave motion will stand."

Ann was on her feet beside Maria, Sylvia and Al Montgomery. Next, the opponents stood. There seemed to be a lot of them but Maria, her eyes darting around the room, broke into a smile.

"We've made it, I think. If more people like you and Sylvia would come to meetings, we'd really get this union into the twentieth century," she added triumphantly

The president banged for silence.

"I have the vote. By 176 votes to 123, Local 357 has amended its instructions to the bargaining committee to say that no contract will be acceptable to the membership without paid maternity leave. Now, let's get on with the rest of the meeting. The guard will untile the doors. . . ."

The Union Pyramid

Local 357 is one of the thousands of unions across Canada. Ann is one of more than three million men and women who make up the Canadian labour movement. In Canada, as in every free country in the world, unions and employers negotiate how much workers will be

Delegates to a Canadian Labour Congress convention vote on a resolution. Union members elect their own leaders, vote on policies at union meetings and send representatives to central organizations and to national or international conventions of their union.

paid, how long they will work and how they will be cared for in sickness and old age. A major part of negotiations is the threat that the company or the union can stop work as a way of backing its point of view. The right to *collective bargaining* is one of those basic freedoms Canadians have learned to cherish, even if, like all freedoms, it sometimes brings costly inconvenience.

Ann's *local union* is part of a larger labour organization with many branches or "locals" across Canada. Some unions are called *international* because they organize workers in both Canada and the United States. The United Steelworkers, with headquarters in Pittsburgh and two hundred thousand members in Canada, is the biggest of the internationals. The International Association of Siderographers, with only four Canadian members, is certainly the smallest. A majority of Canadian unionists now belong to *national* unions with their headquarters and members in Canada. The biggest of the nationals is the 230,000-member Canadian Union of Public Employees.

It is by belonging to a larger national or international union that local unions get their strength. By pooling their funds, union members can support a local which decides to *strike*, or stop work, as part of the bargaining for a contract. The bigger organization has enough money to hire experienced lawyers, experts on industrial safety, or economists like Helen Toyama. Some unions, like the United Auto Workers, which have to deal with a few very large employers, have to do much of their bargaining centrally, although there are usually issues in each plant or factory which local unions must settle.

Like the local union, the larger organization is run democratically. Members elect union officers and an executive to manage the finances and administration of the organization. Union policy conventions meet to plan bargaining strategies. At its convention, Ann's union had agreed to push hard for paid maternity leave.

Some unions in Canada are independent. They are not connected with other unions in the Canadian labour movement. However, Ann's local union is linked to a lot of organizations designed to give members a strong collective voice. Because Ann's union is affiliated with the Canadian Labour Congress (CLC), her local also sends delegates to the provincial labour federation and the local labour council. There are other central labour bodies that are rivals to the two-million-member CLC. The Confederation of National Trade Unions, a Quebec-based body with 220,000 members and the small, nationalistic Confederation of Canadian Unions are two of these. Many Canadian unions even have world-wide connections with international federations. These unions join with unions in the same industry in other countries. The Canadian Labour Congress, for example, is a leading member of the International Confederation of Free Trade Unions, with headquarters in Geneva, Switzerland.

Unions like Ann's may also be affiliated to non-union political organizations. These might include the New Democratic Party, consumer and environmental groups and human rights committees. While most of the money Ann pays as *union dues* is spent by her union and by Local 357, small amounts go to support all the organizations to which her union is affiliated.

Most of the labour news in Canada seems to be made by these larger organizations. That is not surprising. Just as Ann's company, Gamble Industries, protects its interests through national and provincial organizations, her union wants a voice in shaping government policy and public opinion. By supporting political organizations like the New Democratic Party, union members can work for policies which they believe would benefit all Canadians. Business has the same good reason to support its political friends.

However important it is for union leaders to appear on the national news, the real labour news is made at the level of Local 357 and its employer. In Canada, it is there that most contracts are settled. It is the company and the local union that decide whether there will be a strike or whether, as in more than nineteen cases out of twenty, an agreement will be signed without any disruption.

The role of local unions is no accident. Some countries have highly centralized unions. Canadian labour law encourages local *bargaining units* based on employees with a common interest, like sharing the same employer or working in a single factory, mine or office. Some unions, known as *craft unions*, recruit members who share special skills—printers, carpenters, electricians, operating engineers. In contrast, *industrial unions* group all the workers in a single industry whatever their occupation or skill. Workers in automobile and auto parts factories belong to the United Auto Workers, for instance. Conflict between these two kinds of organization is an old problem in Canadian labour circles.

Negotiating a *collective agreement*, or contract, with Gamble Industries is probably the most important single thing Local 357 does for its members. That is why more than the usual handful of members came to the union meeting. The people there knew that their pay, hours of work, vacations, pensions and benefits would all be covered by that contract. Some of them, from harsh experience, knew other features of the contract. If business was poor and the company had to *lay off* workers, the contract would protect those with longer service. Promotion to better jobs would be offered to qualified workers with *seniority*, not to "favourites." Because the company can do anything that is not specifically prevented by the contract, union negotiators add more and more sections as a result of experience. Local 357's contract with Gamble Industries has grown from a couple of mimeographed sheets in 1946 to a fat little booklet of more than a hundred pages.

In Canada, collective bargaining occurs within a very strict framework of laws. If agreement proves difficult, governments provide *mediators*—people skilled in getting opposing sides to settle their arguments. Sometimes, employees in vital services are prevented by law from striking. In those cases, disputes are settled by an indepen-

Once a contract has been negotiated, it must be 'ratified' or approved by union members. This is an important time for the union because once a contract is approved, strikes or lockouts are usually against the law.

dent *arbitrator* who tries to be fair to both sides. However, most Canadian workers have the right, after every effort has been made to get a settlement, to go on *strike*. Similarly, their employer has a right to *lock out* union members who no longer have a contract. In practice, the employer's real weapon is an ability to "take a strike"—to let union members strike until their money is gone and their spirits are bent if not broken. Sometimes, if business is bad, it may even be wise of an employer to let a strike drag on. Of course, employers sometimes cannot afford a strike *or* a settlement.

Local 357, like other unions, had studied business conditions and did not want to strike. It settled for less than its members wanted but more than they had before. It was a compromise for both sides. Now the union and the company had to make the contract work. Next to collective bargaining, the most important thing that a company and its union do together is to make the *grievance procedure* effective.

It was another humid, hot Friday. The air conditioning had broken down and so had just about every other machine in the unit including the computer. Only dreams of the coming weekend kept Ann going. If she ran, she would make it to the bus terminal in time. In an hour, she'd be at her parent's cottage by the lake. Heaven.

Ann's supervisor, Mrs. Dodge, had other concerns. The new orders had to be out by the end of the month. The computer and machinery breakdowns were the last straw. Now everything would have to be sorted by hand. She snapped at an employee she saw slipping back from a coffee break. The company needed the job done and, in Mrs. Dodge's book, the company came first.

"Okay," the supervisor shouted at the workers on the sorting tables. Ann looked up. From Mrs. Dodge's scowl, she knew it was not okay.

"I'm sorry," Mrs. Dodge continued, "but you know these orders have to get out and we'll just have to stay here until the work is done. You'll be paid overtime at the higher rate, and you'll get dinner money. Now let's get the job done."

An operator in a modern, highly automated steel mill. Unions protect the rights of workers who may lose jobs or hard-earned seniority because of new technology. Workers should not pay the full cost of change.

Ann felt a helpless rage. She and the others at her table had been working hard in spite of the heat because they knew the job was urgent. But what was the use? Now she wouldn't get to the cottage until Saturday afternoon. She saw one of the other women get up.

"Where are you going?" Mrs. Dodge demanded.

"If we've got to stay here," the woman answered, "I'm sure you won't mind if I check with Mrs. Moretti, the shop steward." The supervisor nodded.

In a few minutes, Maria Moretti appeared around the partition. In one hand she carried a well-thumbed copy of the collective agreement, in the other, her familiar black handbag. She and Mrs. Dodge disappeared into the supervisor's office.

"Look, Martha," Maria sighed after a few minutes of heated argument, "we aren't reading this section the same way. You say the company has a right to demand overtime in an emergency and I say it isn't an emergency. The end of the month is next Monday, not tonight. If you keep those people working, I'll put in a grievance, and the union will take it all the way to arbitration. That won't give us back the weekend, but it won't look good on your record either. Now isn't there some way to work this out?"

Mrs. Dodge paused for a moment. "I've made a decision, Maria, and I don't see how I can go back on it. With all that has to be done, there is no other way those orders can be ready by Monday night. We'll pay overtime and that's all you're entitled to in the contract."

"Maybe," Maria answered, "but how about this? Why not call them in early on Monday? You know that these are good people but right now they are hot, tired and angry. Their weekend plans are wrecked. On Monday, they'll be cool, fresh and rested. The air conditioning and the computer may be working. Anyway, you'll have given the twenty-four hours' notice the contract requires for normal overtime. You'll get the job done. And no grievance."

Martha Dodge thought for a moment. The she smiled, "Thanks, Maria. It's a deal."

"Us" and "Them"

Grievances can cover almost any imaginable complaint a worker can make, from the silly to the very serious. Veteran labour negotiators know that unresolved grievances cause more strikes than do demands for more pay. An unresolved grievance will sent both parties to the bargaining table feeling aggressive.

Every collective agreement has a section showing how grievances will be handled. What starts with a supervisor like Mrs. Dodge and a shop steward (the union official closest to the workers) like Maria Moretti could go all the way to independent *arbitrators* hearing a case argued by lawyers. Grievance procedure is one of the important ways that both the company and the union protect individual workers' rights.

Like all active unions, Local 357 was involved in much more than bargaining and grievances. An education committee organized courses for new shop stewards. It also worked with a local community college to develop a labour studies program. A monthly newspaper, handed out at the factory gates, printed reports from union officers, chatty articles from the departments in Gamble Industries and an occasional barbed political commentary from Jack McLeod. As a respected community organization, Local 357 took part in the city's United Appeal campaign. Thanks to members like Bill Scranton, it sponsored minor league hockey. The union was proud that one of its members sat on city council.

Of course, like other organizations, Local 357 depended on a few loyal regulars to carry most of the burden. Ann often heard Maria complain that younger members took the union for granted. Yet the Local's members did come together when they were needed. Most had come to the meeting to discuss the contract. They always came out for the annual children's Christmas party, a popular tradition in the union. Then there was the city transit strike.

It seemed to Ann that no one had a good word to say for the strikers. Her parents were furious. Newspaper and radio editorials blasted the drivers for hurting business. Some of Ann's friends sneered at them for demanding more money. Almost in spite of herself, Ann took the strikers' side. Maybe, she argued, the transit commission was being unreasonable. Then she found that most of her fellow workers were also cheering for the drivers. For the first time, Ann began to think of the strikers as "us" and the transit commission, the newspaper and radio editors, perhaps even her own parents, as "them." It was a new feeling.

The Adversary System

The sense of "us" and "them" comes as a surprise to most Canadians, who are taught that there should not be differences between

Some union members are not allowed to strike. These Ontario hospital workers have met with Shirley Carr, a vice-president of the Canadian Labour Congress to start a campaign for public support for a "catch up" of their lagging wages.

rich and poor or between workers and their employers. Yet differences exist and are seen every day. Moreover, conflict is built into Canadian industrial relations. Experts call it an *adversary system*. When Gamble Industries and Local 357 bargain, it is hoped that out of their conflict will come a fair contract. In the same way, prosecution and defence lawyers compete in a court of law, government and opposition members debate in Parliament, and a buyer and a seller haggle over a fair price.

Many Canadians do not like this kind of struggle, with the battle lines drawn between "us" and "them." Many individuals believe that they can get a better deal by negotiating with an employer on their own. Business executives, managers, sales personnel normally do not look to unions for help in setting their salaries. At the other end of the scale, millions of Canada's poorest people have never joined unions, sometimes because the law or their job makes it impossible. In Canada, most union members are somewhere in the middle, neither rich nor poor.

On the whole, unions in Canada are not as strong or influential as they are in countries such as Sweden or West Germany. There, unions influence government policies. Union representatives help to manage some of the biggest companies. In Canada, only a third of the workers are organized; in some European countries, unions include two-thirds to four-fifths of all workers.

Many people exaggerate the wealth of unions in Canada. If all the country's unions put their money into a single account, it would add up to just over a billion dollars. Unions try to sound stronger and more united than they really are. They try to persuade their members to understand the importance of union "solidarity." Not only is that the title of the most popular union song, it becomes a part of a good unionist's life.

When they go shopping, loyal union members check for the *union label*—a mark that shows that the product was made by fellow union workers. A union on strike posts *pickets* at the entrance to the work place. The picketers, usually wearing or carrying placards, show that a labour dispute is in progress. No good unionist ever crosses any picket line willingly—though sometimes a contract leaves a worker no choice. Anyone who takes a striker's job becomes, in the eyes of a unionist, the lowest of the low—a *scab*.

At her first meeting, Ann had felt uncomfortable at hearing expressions like "Brothers and Sisters." She was puzzled by old-fashioned terms like "tiling the doors." Yet she was impressed when old Jack McLeod spoke of the idealism that had started Local 357. There were things she liked about her union and there were other features that annoyed her. At lunch break one day, Ann noticed that McLeod was sitting alone at the back of the cafeteria.

"Would you mind if I joined you?" she asked.

"It would be a privilege," he smiled, rising for an old-fashioned bow. "I will even put off lighting my pipe in honour of the occasion."

"No, please, go ahead." Ann felt embarrassed but she continued. "It's just that I heard you the other night at the meeting, and I wondered what it was really like when the union got started."

"Oh, that's ancient history now," McLeod laughed. "People like me live too much in the past. What excites me is the kind of future you will see."

"But there are so many traditions and old-fashioned things about the union," Ann persisted. "I wonder about some of them. And why

is there so much bitterness when I don't see that much to complain about?''

McLeod's pipe had begun to draw. "Well," he paused for a moment, "I suppose it's a matter of experience." He puffed again. "What we are today is the result of what we have experienced for generations, long before even I was born." He looked at her with a wink. "Some of our memories should be forgotten. Take Gamble Industries. It isn't the same place as it was under Old Man Gamble. And the union has changed too. Just imagine me getting up and arguing for maternity leave! When I started here, a woman was fired for getting married.''

McLeod looked around the cafeteria, "You know, Ann," he continued, "history made this Canadian labour movement, warts and all. You're right. If you want to understand labour and management, history is where you start.''

First Unions

It was almost 11P.M. before the crowd could finally see the approaching train. Moonlight caught the stiff plumes of steam rising from the three big locomotives as they crossed the bridge over the frozen Moira River. In the station yard, the people stood silent, a black mass on the glistening snow.

For three bitterly cold days, Belleville had defied the Grand Trunk Railway. A few hundred men had taken up the cause of the striking locomotive engineers. At Stratford, Brockville and Toronto, Canada's biggest corporation had crushed its enemies. Now, on January 2, 1877, it was Belleville's turn. The soldiers were coming.

Three hundred yards from the station, the long train braked to a stop, sparks hissing from the great driving wheels. At once, dark-clad militiamen leaped from the cabs. More poured from the passenger cars. Curt orders pulled them into line. A few boys who had raced forward to hurl frozen snowballs at the locomotives fled back to the shelter of the crowd. Now the troops, their rifles tipped with long, glinting bayonets, advanced. The crowd fell back, murmuring in angry frustration. Their long, cold struggle was lost.

People came to Canada despite its reputation for harsh winters and short summers. They wanted a chance for the wealth and freedom they could never expect in the Old World. The claim that anyone could get rich in Canada had just enough truth to make it convincing. In 1885, more than half of Canada's 186 leading factory owners had begun as immigrants, many of them without a penny.

Pioneers were promised that work digging canals or building railways would give them the money to start their own business or farm. Skilled carpenters, shoemakers and printers were always in demand.

In a land of opportunity, anyone who remained a hired person seemed a failure. Failures or not, employees had few rights. Slavery had been abolished in British colonies in 1800, but until 1877, a worker could be jailed for quitting a job without an employer's permission. Few working men could vote in elections before 1885; women had another thirty years to wait.

In good times, Canadian workers were much better off than friends or relatives in the Old World. An unskilled labourer worked sixty hours a week in 1867 and earned a dollar a day. A skilled worker was paid two or three times as much, but women and children earned less than a man. A family could afford a home with two or three rooms, enough clothes and a dull but filling diet of potatoes, bread and cheese. No employer dreamed of offering paid holidays, and only governments and railway companies even considered retirement pensions. For help with medical bills and funeral expenses, working people turned to neighbours or to fraternal orders like the Hibernians, St. Andrew's Society or the Loyal Orange Lodge.

Good times never lasted. Working people lived on the edge of survival. In winter, employers usually cut wages and fired workers just as the price of food and fuel began to climb. In bad times, summer was no better. Jobs and savings disappeared. Men tramped the roads looking for work. They lined up at soup kitchens. Sickness, injury and old age were disasters for people who earned too little to save any money. Not until 1887 did any government in Canada pass laws to make factory owners provide safe working conditions. Although provinces started "poorhouses," an official in Peterborough reported in 1892 that old people were put in jail to keep them from starving.

The Earliest Unions

Unions in Canada began as a way to protect workers in a trade or industry from the financial disasters of sickness or unemployment. One of the oldest unions was the Toronto Typographical Union, formed in 1833. It is now Local 91 of the International Typographical Union. As their motto, the Toronto printers boasted that they were "United to Support, not Combined to Injure."

Few Canadian workers earned enough money or had jobs that were dependable enough to keep a union going even as a kind of insurance club. Those who did were those who had special skills or abilities—printers who had to be well educated and nimble-fingered, dock workers, who had to be strong as well as honest and dependable.

Even their unions did not last long. Bad times emptied their treasuries and sent members looking elsewhere for work. Or the unions fell foul of employers when they started trying to do more for their members. Printers, shoemakers, glass-blowers, barrel-makers might meet to talk about hiring a doctor or arranging a banquet but the talk must soon have turned to wages. Talk led to action.

In the 1860s, dockworkers in Saint John, New Brunswick, "ruled the port with a rod of iron." They quit work to attend any member's funeral and notified employers of their desired wage rates through newspaper advertisements. Ironmoulders and other highly skilled workers in Toronto, Hamilton and Montreal set their own wages. An old custom among glass-blowers was to do little work on "Blue Monday" so that they could recover from the weekend. In return, glass-blowers promised to "give her Hell" the rest of the week.

Employers naturally disliked such independence. Unions, in legal language, were "combinations in restraint of trade" and illegal. Even worse, unions turned society upside down. Workers were expected to take orders, not to give them. If two or more workers got together to plan a strike, they were "criminal conspirators" subject to a stiff prison term. Judges were more likely to agree with employers than with rebellious workers. The wonder is not that unions were small and short-lived in Canada but that any survived at all.

But survive they did because a few brave individuals took the risk of standing up for their fellow workers. Workers turned to unions when they saw that they could never hope to become their own masters. The era of the workshop with a master and a few helpers changed to the age of the factory, with hundreds or even thousands of workers employed in a single company. Unions also developed in Canada because they were growing in Great Britain and the United States. In the 1850s, railways made the movement of people and ideas easier. Canadians learned about wages and working conditions in cities like Boston, New York and Philadelphia. When times were hard, skilled workers wrapped up their tools and "tramped." Often they would join unions in American cities and they brought the idea home to Canada.

"New-Model" Unions

The railway age brought thousands of skilled workers from Britain. In 1853, English workers formed a new union, the Amalgamated Society of Engineers (ASE). Like many other unions, it took on employers and was beaten. There was one difference. Unlike other unions, the Amalgamated survived to fight again. People asked how this "new-model" unionism worked. The answer was plain. The ASE organized only highly-skilled workers. It collected high dues and it paid members during a strike. The union was tightly controlled by its leaders. The ASE was tough, business-like and realistic. New-model unionism spread in England and the United States. It could do nothing for ill-paid, unskilled workers. It gave well-paid skilled workers a fighting chance.

In 1863, an American new-model union, the Iron Moulders, formed locals in Canada. Other Canadians asked to join American unions. The Americans agreed. As usual, the arguments were practical. If Canadian printers or iron moulders belonged to the same union as Americans, they would not willingly "break a strike." Canadian workers also wanted protection from American strikebreakers or

Montreal carpenters and other unions gather outside the city's armouries in 1893 for the annual Labour Day parade. Skilled workers in both French and English Canada had begun to form unions in the 1860s. By 1893, they were common in big cities.

"Buffalos." (Canadian employers often went to that New York border city to hire workers.)

The kind of labour organization that won a foothold in Canada in the 1860s is called "craft unionism." It was built on the skill, pride and financial security of highly-trained workers. Their main fear was that hard-earned skills would be outdated by new machines or that employers would hire helpers and unskilled workers to dilute the craftsmen. For thirty years, the biggest issue for the Iron Moulders' Union was the right of its members to hire their own "bucks," or helpers.

With Confederation in 1867, Canadians became fervent organizers of clubs, sporting teams and labour unions. Booming prosperity spurred the enthusiasm. In the United States, a national labour organization launched a campaign for the eight-hour day. In Hamilton, a city-wide labour organization began to meet and debate reforming ideas. One of their proposals was a campaign for the more modest British labour goal of a nine-hour day. Newly formed "trades assemblies" in Toronto, Montreal and smaller Canadian cities agreed to cooperate. Hamilton employers at first agreed to shorter hours, provided the campaign succeeded across Canada. On second thought, they fought back, firing workers who joined the campaign. In Galt (now Cambridge) a factory owner forced his workers to sign a statement opposing shorter hours. Those who refused would lose their jobs. In Toronto, the printers' union jumped the gun by launching a strike against their old enemy, George Brown, the Liberal publisher of the Toronto *Globe*. Montreal workers were too weakly organized to carry their share of the campaign. Canadian labour's first big effort was a failure.

That was not the end of the story. George Brown, who hated unions, had his striking printers arrested for their "criminal conspiracy" in planning a strike. By 1872, many Canadians thought such a law was outdated. Ten thousand people gathered in Toronto for a peaceful protest. Canada's prime minister, Sir John A. Macdonald, was impressed. He also saw that he could embarrass his leading Liberal opponent. All at once, Canada's Parliament was invited to pass the same Trade Unions Act a British Liberal government had adopted a year before. To George Brown's fury, his fellow Liberals agreed to the new law. Sir John A. Macdonald and the Conservatives could take the credit of making labour unions legal in Canada.

Though Macdonald's laws strictly limited unions with harsh

penalties for picketing and other strike tactics, many union members were pleased. In 1873, Toronto's labour leaders celebrated by trying to establish a nation-wide Canadian Labour Union. Travel costs made it impossible for delegates from outside Ontario to attend. However, a great many of the subjects discussed that September at Canada's first labour convention still interest unionists more than a hundred years later: the problems of organizing, the lack of apprenticeship training, the need to elect labour supporters to Parliament. Happily, some concerns have changed. Delegates then insisted that children under ten years of age should no longer work in factories.

A few workingmen did win elections. In 1874, an Ottawa printer, Daniel O'Donoghue, ran in a provincial by-election and, to most people's surprise, he won. Later, Lord Dufferin, the governor-general, asked O'Donoghue whom he represented. "Your Excellency", he answered, "I represent the rag, tag and bobtail."

The early 1870s seemed to promise Canadian labour a bright future. True, there were only a few thousand union members, most of them in Ontario cities like Toronto, Hamilton, Ottawa and Brantford, but the movement was growing. Suddenly, the mood changed. By late 1874, Canada was in a deep economic depression. By 1877, the Canadian Labour Union had collapsed because no one could afford to come to the convention. Hundreds of businesses were ruined. Others slashed wages to try to compete. Unions that tried to protect their members failed. How could a strike succeed when thousands of workers, skilled and unskilled, pleaded for any job, however ill-paid?

There were rare exceptions. The Brotherhood of Locomotive Engineers, created in 1860, was the most cautious of new-model unions. Even railway companies admitted that the Brotherhood was useful, providing its members with insurance and punishing them for drunkenness and other misbehaviour. Most of the engineers on the Grand Trunk, Canada's biggest railway, were union members.

In 1876, a Grand Trunk official who hated any kind of union decided to drive out the Brotherhood. He cut the engineers' wages and fired anyone who complained. Even the cautious Brotherhood, after months of hunting for a peaceful settlement, had to fight back. On Christmas Eve the engineers stopped work. From Sarnia, Ontario, to Richmond, Quebec, Canada's main railway was paralyzed. In most places, strikers gave up after a few arrests. At Belleville, angry citizens helped the strikers blockade the railway. Just as soldiers arrived from Toronto to drive the people from the station, the Grand Trunk

When people at Belleville blockaded the line of the hated Grand Trunk Railway to support striking engineers, the local authorities sent to Toronto for militia. By the time they arrived, the company had decided to settle the strike.

management agreed to negotiate. The bid to destroy the union had cost too much.

Can Macdonald's National Policy Help?

During those grim depression years, Canadian workers looked for any idea that might bring back good times. The most popular suggestion came from Sir John A. Macdonald, the Conservative leader. In 1878, he had returned to power with a program he called his "National Policy." Its main idea was that the government should put a heavy tax or *tariff* on most things brought into the country. The tariff would make Canadian-made articles less expensive to buy than foreign-made items even if the cost of producing them was higher or the quality was lower. That meant new factories and more jobs for workers.

Macdonald's idea of a tariff was bitterly debated. It raised the cost of living and it did little for areas of Canada where there was no manufacturing. On the other hand, tariffs helped Canadian industry and they seemed to help workers too. Another feature of Macdonald's National Policy was more immigration. This was less pleasing to workers. Instead of giving Canadians higher wages, the government helped employers to get more workers from abroad.

In the short run, the National Policy brought back some of the old prosperity. Manufacturers built new factories and bought more of the machinery that threatened old skills. Good times and the threat to skilled workers revived labour organization especially in Ontario and Quebec. However, the growth of craft unions was overshadowed when a new movement burst on the Canadian scene.

The Knights of Labor

The Holy and Noble Order of the Knights of Labor had begun in Philadelphia in 1868. Its members argued that new-model unionism did nothing for most working people. The Knights would be open to everyone, men and women, skilled and unskilled. Only "proven enemies of labor," lawyers, bankers and the liquor industry, were kept out. To survive employer hostility, the Knights became a secret society. Five asterisks, * * * * *, concealed the name. Until 1879, when Terence V. Powderly became General Master Workman, the Knights grew very slowly. Powderly relaxed the secrecy rule and diluted some of the Knights' strict principles. Suddenly, membership soared.

In 1881, a few Hamilton workers formed the first Canadian "assembly." Like Americans, Canadians liked the Knights' mixture of idealism and caution. The Knights of Labor proclaimed the worth and dignity of working people, the evils of monopoly and the dream of someday creating a "co-operative commonwealth." Meanwhile, Powderly insisted, the Knights must co-operate with employers and each other. Great reforms were needed but they would come only through patience and education. Even some wealthy and influential Canadians could support that kind of radical message. Because the Knights ignored the barriers of craft unionism, their "mixed assemblies" were ideal for towns too small to support even a single local union of carpenters or machinists.

During the 1880s, the Knights of Labor spread into almost every part of Canada. In many towns, the history of unionism begins with an assembly of Knights. At first Catholic bishops tried to keep the Order out of Quebec because they saw it as a dangerous secret society. American Catholic leaders helped to change their minds. So did the fact that Powderly was a devout Catholic. Many French-Canadian workers joined, and by 1887 the Knights boasted twenty thousand Canadian members. Many thousands more had belonged for short periods.

That was part of the problem. Floods of new members could not be taught the Order's philosophy and its cautious approach. When American Knights won a dramatic strike against a brutal American railroad owner, hundreds of thousands of fellow workers joined the organization. Many of them went on strike or were fired. Harrassed and over-worked, Powderly ordered all recruiting stopped. Local assemblies quarrelled with the older craft unions. In 1886, the craft unions organized the rival American Federation of Labor (AFL). Public opinion turned against the Knights when the Order was unfairly blamed for an 1887 riot in Chicago.

To the Canadian Knights, these were distant battles. The Order's enthusiasm for education produced some of Canada's liveliest labour newspapers. The Knights' eagerness for reform led to a clash of radical opinions. For the first time Canadians eagerly discussed the need for co-operatives, the fairness of taxing the incomes of the wealthy, or the benefits of socialism. Because the Knights showed the political strength of organized workers, Ontario and Quebec governments adopted factory safety laws. More and more workingmen won the right to vote. Toronto's annual exhibition cashed in on the new enthusiasm. In 1886, it proclaimed that the first Monday in September would be "Labour Day." Union members could enter free.

Canadian Knights also had problems. Against their will, members had to strike, usually because employers refused to tolerate even so cautious an organization. After a short strike in 1886, public opinion forced the owner of Toronto's streetcar company to allow his drivers to belong to a union. He fought back by firing Knights one by one.

Vigorous debate could also shatter local assemblies of the Order. Hamilton's strong organization of Knights was split by an internal argument. Toronto and Ottawa district assemblies shared the same fate. By the 1980s, the Holy and Noble Order was almost dead in the United States and it was dying in Canada. It lasted longest in French Canada as the *Chevaliers du Travail*.

It was the craft unions, not their exciting competitors, who lived on. Leaders like Sam Gompers, president of the new American Federation of Labor, argued that the Knights had proved three golden rules for union organizers. First, it was impossible to organize ill-paid, unskilled workers. Second, discussing politics and new ideas was more trouble than it was worth. Third, dual unionism (two unions competing for members in the same craft or industry) was fatal. Much of the labour history of the United States and Canada would be based on challenging these three principles.

Leaders and delegates of the Trades and Labour Congress of Canada, meeting at Winnipeg in 1897. Among those in the front row, with a shock of white hair and a long beard, is Dan O'Donoghue, sometimes called the "Father of Canadian Labour."

The Parliament of Canadian Labour

In Canada, the Knights and the craft unions had not quarrelled. Instead, they worked together to rebuild a national organization. In 1883 and again in 1886 Toronto labour leaders invited unions from other cities to send delegates to a national congress. From 1886 the Trades and Labour Congress of Canada (TLC) would meet every year until 1956 when it became the biggest partner in forming the Canadian Labour Congress (CLC).

In what it proudly called "the Parliament of Canada Labour," the TLC put together a list of reforms that would help working people. Delegates called for shorter hours of work and inspectors to enforce the factory safety laws. They wanted free education for all children at a time when many parents had to pay school fees. Labour delegates wanted a more democratic Canada. They called for an end to the Senate, with its privileged members appointed for life. Some labour demands were more selfish. Because employers used immigrants to take jobs from Canadian workers, the TLC wanted immigration tightly controlled. Racial prejudice helped explain why the Congress wanted Oriental immigrants kept out altogether.

Leaders of the Trades and Labour Congress soon began to hold annual meetings with politicians in Ottawa and the provincial capitals. At first, the union men were overawed by the chance to speak with cabinet ministers and high officials. Later, when their requests, were largely ignored, some unionists grew scornful of these "cap in hand" sessions. The answer, they insisted, was for union members themselves to join the lawyers, farmers and businessmen who filled the Canadian Parliament and provincial legislatures. Again and again TLC conventions heard delegates call for labour to start its own political party with a distinctive program. It sometimes seemed that labour's only gain came in 1894 when Labour Day finally became an official holiday.

Yet, for every radical voice, there were two that urged caution. Unions spoke for a small minority of workers. Even union members refused to see their employer as an enemy. Men like Phillips Thompson, a Toronto newspaperman who wanted a "labour reform" party, were outnumbered by loyal Liberals and Conservatives. "It would be

Winnipeg Painters on parade in 1914. Labour Day began in Canada in 1886. In 1894, it became a statutory holiday, to recognize the contribution of working people to Canadian prosperity. Often employers paid for picnics and entertainment.

as easy to move Hamilton Bay and put it upon the mountain," warned a TLC delegate, "as to get a Conservative to vote for a Liberal Labour Candidate or a Liberal Workingman to vote for a Conservative Labour Candidate."*

A New Prosperity

From 1873 to 1896, Canadians had built thousands of factories, linked the Atlantic and the Pacific with a railway and grown in wealth and population. Few people noticed. They remembered only years of hard times. Without warning, in 1896 the mood changed. Maybe it was the discovery of gold in South Africa or an unusual run of good weather in western Canada. It might even have been the new Liberal government in Ottawa under Wilfrid Laurier. Suddenly, Canadians felt themselves afloat on a wave of prosperity. Factories expanded. Americans, looking for a place to invest their money, spent it on branch plants and mines in Canada. A tide of settlers began to fill the western prairies. Now a single transcontinental railway was not enough. Canada would have three of them.

Canadian workers shared the mood but they saw few of the benefits. Immigrants, surging into Canada, became cheap labour for the expanding industries and mines. Many of the newcomers brought their own experience of unions in Great Britain and other European countries. Some of them were even less willing than Canadians to put up with harsh conditions or unfair treatment. Companies, desperate to find skilled workers, had to hire the well-trained British craftsmen, but some employers soon put up signs saying: "No English Need Apply."

The United States was an even bigger influence than Britain on Canadian workers. For one thing, Canadians could still cross the border easily to find work and they saw how Sam Gompers's craft unions were winning better pay for skilled carpenters, printers and machinists. Gompers, too, was worried about Canada. If American companies went north to find cheaper workers, members of his American Federation of Labour could lose their jobs. Unions in Canada seemed to be asleep.

In 1899, Gompers hired a Hamilton carpenter, John Flett, as a full-time union organizer. Flett was a whirlwind success. He organized local unions, got them together in local labour councils and found

---

* The word "Liberal" has been substituted for the old equivalent, "Reform."

A raft on the Ottawa river. Canadian development was only possible through the skill and energy of thousands of workers. Loggers like these chopped trees, drove logs down the icy streams of the spring break-up and then piloted huge rafts of squared timber down river to Quebec.

part-time organizers to carry on the work. It was almost like the Knights of Labor crusade, but this time it was tightly managed by the conservative international unions of Gompers's American Federation of Labor.

Employers, politicians and other unionists objected to the invasion. In 1898, the Trades and Labour Congress had asked the Americans for help, but now its leaders grew nervous. The president, Ralph Smith, was a Liberal-Labour member of Parliament from British Columbia. In 1901, he urged the Congress convention to become a Canadian Federation of Labour, independent of Gompers's organization. That would probably mean that Canadian workers would have to separate from their international unions.

The debate was delayed for a year, until the TLC's 1902 convention at Berlin (now Kitchener). Both sides organized. Flett urged his new locals to send delegates. Labour radicals came in force, suspicious that Ralph Smith was trying to serve the Liberal party, not labour. Others complained that the TLC was run by delegates like Dan O'Donoghue who represented non-existent Knights of Labor assemblies. In the showdown, Smith and his followers were overwhelmed. In a key vote, delegates decided to expel as "dual unions" any Canadian organization that tried to compete with an international union.

At the time, the Berlin meeting affected only a few thousand Canadian workers. The TLC was a tiny organization. Its secretary, Paddy Draper, proudly boasted that he employed two part-time office workers. The expelled unions formed a Canadian Federation of Labour, but it was clear that most Canadian workers did not really want national unions. If they had they could have rejected the internationals. They did not do so. For the next seventy years, most Canadian workers chose to support American-based unions. They wanted all the strength and experience they could get because they wanted a North American standard of living.

Employers, newspaper editors and politicians were indignant at the TLC's decision. In 1900, the Laurier government had even created a small department of labour as a gesture towards union members. Now, the government felt rebuffed. Senators, led by James Lougheed from Alberta, almost pushed through a law that threatened two years in jail for any American labour organizer causing a strike in Canada. Employers could use Anti-American feeling when they launched a campaign against the growing craft unions in 1903.

Yet many of those employers were American. Canadian manufacturers joined American-based organizations. Even their anti-union tactics, like forming city-wide employer associations, "blacklisting" union leaders so that no one would hire them, or locking out workers in an entire industry to break their union, were borrowed because they had worked well in American cities.

In time, both the government and employers found that there were benefits in the conservative "business" unionism supported by Samuel Gompers. Skilled workers, for the most part, were moderate and even cautious in their views. They wanted stability as much as their employers. Canadian businessmen could not pretend to like unions but they gradually learned that some kinds of union were easier to work with than others.

Angry Men

In the woods, seven long blasts on the steam whistle meant only one thing: a deadly accident. Before the last echo had faded across the hills, men had raced to the scene. A "bucker," cutting the big trees into sections, had accidentally kicked a wedge. Now, two huge logs pinned him to the ground like an ant.

For an hour the man lay in agony while the loggers struggled to lever him free. By the time he was lifted in a blanket and carried down the path to the road, he lay white-faced and silent. The cook's wagon was harnessed and waiting when the little party reached the trail.

"He'll never make it to town," the foreman grunted as he watched the old Bain wagon jolt down the rough bush road, "and he still owes us most of his railway fare."

In the bunkhouse, a logger bundled up the man's few possessions. He had come only two weeks before, pitching his blankets into the empty bunk behind the door—one of the "muzzle-loaders" you could only climb into over the end. Like others in the shack, the newcomer had worked in mines from Alberta to Colorado. He had laid track for the Canadian Northern, worked on threshing crews but, in the woods, he had been a greenhorn. Now he would pay the price for his inexperience with his legs—or his life.

The others had called him "Mac," scorning his long Polish name. Once, during a break between the endless card games, he had tried to show them his real name, painfully printed on a red membership card of the Industrial Workers of the World.

"Cut out that union stuff, Mac," a logger had called out, "or I'll show you what we did to the last foreign-speaking Wobbly we had here."

Land of Immigrants

The union idea spread across Canada but always it worked best for those with scarce skills. In 1859, when Victoria was hardly more than an outpost on the Pacific coast, its "practical bakers" had banded together. Printers and carpenters were not far behind. A continent away, in St. John's, Newfoundland, seal-skinners decided to protect their skill and their high pay with a union.

These were exceptions. Most men could sell only their strength and the kind of skill with an axe, a paddle or a team of horses that was as common as the ability to drive a car would be today. Before the age of machinery, Canada needed huge armies of such men. The timber wealth of New Brunswick and of Upper and Lower Canada was worthless without thousands of lumbermen willing to winter in the shanties and bring down the great log drives in the spring. Thousands of Irish immigrants, fleeing poverty and famine at home, became "canallers" in Canada, digging out the big locks that connected the Great Lakes and the St. Lawrence River. Later waves of immigrants became the "navvies" who built Canada's railways.

City people at the time knew very little about the men who were actually turning the wilderness into the kind of country we know today. We see the "bunkhouse men" through their eyes, as they poured into town at the end of the season, flush with money and looking for fun. Voyageurs, lumberjacks and construction "stiffs" seem happy-go-lucky and carefree, content to squander their money and return penniless to the hard but healthy life of the camps.

Life in the camps was indeed hard, and it could be anything but healthy. Lumberjacks were soaked in icy water for days on end during the drives and paid the price in arthritis and rheumatism. Accidents in building the Canadian Pacific left thousands dead or maimed for life.

When you next look at a railway or a canal, remember that the work was done by men using picks and shovels with a lot of help from teams of horses. The work was divided among small contractors, each of whom agreed to do a tiny part of the job—clearing trees, filling a swamp, cutting through a rock face. Each contractor borrowed money for an "outfit," hired men and horses, and set out to do the job. Some contractors went on to make fortunes. Others failed, sometimes leaving their men unpaid after months of hard work.

To a newcomer, wages on a contract labour gang looked good. No one explained the full costs. Railway contracts in the early 1900s paid $2 for a day's work, but they charged $1 a day for board, including Sundays when no work was done. Each man paid a $1 a month for medical care, though the doctor might be miles away. Boots, clothes and tobacco were available from the van or camp store at prices the contractor set. A worker repaid the cost of his own transportation and he might also have to pay a fee to an employment agency.

Contractors might try to feed and house their men as cheaply as they could, but the wiser operators knew that well-fed, contented men worked harder. Horrifying reports from the railway camps forced governments to appoint inspectors. Still, whether or not the bunk-house men were well-treated, they had few rights. In 1885, after months without pay, men building the Canadian Pacific Railway through the Rocky Mountains finally went on strike. Inspector Sam Steele of the North West Mounted Police arrested the strike leaders and sent them to jail in Calgary.

In his National Policy, Sir John A. Macdonald had forseen the need for a huge pool of labour to develop Canada. Massive immigration would provide workers and consumers; it would also ensure that Canadian workers could not use shortage of manpower as an argument for higher wages. At least until 1896, however, the government's immigration policy was a failure. Immigrants were outnumbered by Canadians fleeing their depression-wracked country for the United States.

To complete the mountain sections of the Canadian Pacific Railway, the government allowed the company to hire workers in China. The Chinese labourers endured harsh conditions while they helped complete the line, and afterwards many of them decided to stay in British Columbia. Some ruthless employers used them and later immigrants from Japan and India as cheap labour. White workers saw the Asian immigrants as a threat to their standard of living. Instead of making common cause with them, they began organizing unions and political associations to drive them out of Canada.

When the Canadian government encouraged immigration, it usually held out the promise that newcomers could become farmers and landowners as they never could in the old world. Immigrants worked on railway construction or in the woods to earn enough money to buy a farm or to set up as a small contractor. Another kind of labour was more permanent. Mining coal had begun in Nova Scotia when ships changed from sail to steam engines. It started on Vancouver Island to serve the British warships based near Victoria. Railway developers hunted for coal and other minerals as a source of fuel for their engines and freight for their trains. Mining needed miners.

The Western Federation of Miners was as tough and uncompromising as the mine owners it faced in northern and western Canada. Miners lived harsh and dangerous lives and the experience made them some of Canada's most radical union members.

A Miner's Life

Miners are tough, clannish people, doing a dirty, dangerous and highly skilled job. Mine owners tried to treat them as independent contractors, paying them not by the hour but by the amount of coal they delivered to the surface. In fact, miners knew that the owners had all the advantages. The owners controlled the weigh scales and they could decide to pay less if they thought the coal was of poor quality. Since most mines were far from towns, miners and their families rented their homes from the mining company. In Cape Breton, miners called the company stores where they bought their supplies "pluck-me"'s. Alex McGillivray, a Nova Scotia miner, told a Royal Commission in 1889 that in his best month he had earned $35.13, working from 6:00 A.M. to 5:30 P.M. By the time he had paid his bill at the company store, his rent and taxes and had bought the dynamite he needed for his work, he had nothing left.

What is more, McGillivray was a union man. In many countries, miners were among the first workers to form unions. In 1879, angry after their second pay-cut in a year, a few miners at Springhill, Nova Scotia, quietly slipped out to meet in a nearby forest. From their secret meeting came the Provincial Workmen's Association (PWA). Although mine owners fought it by every method they knew, the PWA survived. For one thing, most Nova Scotia mine owners were small operators and easily divided. The new Association was also moderate in its demands. Nova Scotia's Liberal party saw the PWA as an avenue to workers' votes. Miners like McGillivray had low wages, but he and his fellow workers had some of the best mining laws anywhere. Nova Scotia miners could hire their own "tallyman" to check the weigh scales. Miners could become mine inspectors. Employers learned that the PWA could help them keep their miners working. When the big Dominion Coal Company bought out the smaller operators, it continued to collect union dues and hand them to the PWA. That was one way to remind the union that the company now controlled its existence.

On Vancouver Island, on the other side of Canada, there was no PWA. Coal mining was developed by a single man, James Dunsmuir, with money invested by officers of the Royal Navy. Dunsmuir was bold, ambitious—and a tyrant. He forced miners to live in his shacks and buy from his store. When miners complained that Dunsmuir's weigh scale cheated them by ten percent, Dunsmuir ordered the men and their families out of their homes. When the miners refused to budge, Dunsmuir persuaded his naval friends to send a warship. Dunsmuir swore that his miners would never organize a union as long as he lived, and he kept his promise.

Many British Columbians admired men like Dunsmuir. They might sympathize with women and children driven from their homes but the miners, after all, had threatened the rights of businessmen to do as they pleased. Other people saw the dispute differently. British Columbia attracted people with new and disturbing ideas. The discontent that moved people from older, more staid communities did not die when they found that their new Garden of Eden was controlled by men like Dunsmuir. Socialists, who claimed that capitalism was greedy and cruel, needed no better argument than James Dunsmuir and his mines. From a workforce that was never more than three thousand, 326 miners died from accidents between 1879 and 1889.

Dunsmuir was not unique. Across the West in both Canada and the United States, a few tough, shrewd men tended to get to the top. Often they had started from the same humble origins as the men they hired. They had no sympathy for others who, they felt, had failed in the race for wealth and power. Union organizers met the same ruthlessness as business competitors. Unions like the Western Federation of Miners and their leaders fought their battles against militia, police and merciless employers. Unionists bred in such struggles had contempt for the cautious craft unionists of the American Federation of Labor. Workers who had done a dozen jobs, from driving spikes to running a thresher, despised arguments about whether a carpenter or a plumber could bore a hole. The only difference that mattered was between worker and boss.

This tough union philosophy came to Canada in the 1890s when American investors developed new mines in the Kootenay region of British Columbia. Veteran hard-rock miners, already members of the Western Federation of Miners, entered the region. When the Canadian Pacific Railway opened a new line through the Crowsnest Pass in 1897, more mines opened. Workers in the interior and on Vancouver Island began to elect their own members to the British Columbia legislature. In 1902, the first two members elected as "socialists" anywhere in the British Empire took their places in the British Columbia assembly.

Discontent may seem surprising when Canada appeared to be booming. Everywhere, factories were busy with orders. The prairies filled with settlers. In fifteen years, Winnipeg grew from 25,000 to 250,000 people. Vancouver was close behind. Some Canadians became enormously rich. Preachers warned that too much luxury would destroy Canada's moral fibre. The warning hardly applied to workers. Prosperity did not reach the bunkhouses or the city slums. The poor stayed poor. Immigrants competed for the new jobs. Employers preferred newcomers because they could be paid less. Labour conflict became violent. In 1902, when the United Brotherhood of Railway Employees tried to organize CPR workers in British Columbia, a union leader was shot. He turned out to be a police spy. During transit strikes at Toronto, Hamilton and London, huge crowds attacked the cars when companies tried to continue operations. Soldiers guarded the streets. At Hamilton, cavalry charged the crowd with swords drawn. In 1906, a clash between strikers and private police at the little Quebec lumber town of Buckingham left three men dead.

Mackenzie King's Department of Labour

The Laurier government found one answer for labour conflict: William Lyon Mackenzie King. In 1900, a new federal Department of Labour was created to study wages and working conditions and, when

William Lyon Mackenzie King campaigns for election in 1908. As the author of the Industrial Disputes Investigation Act, King had won a world-wide reputation as an expert on strikes. Now he would be Canada's first Minister of Labour.

possible, to solve disputes between workers and employers. King was its first official.

Mackenzie King was highly educated, a little fussy and very good at settling quarrels. Reasonable people, he believed, could solve any dispute if they could only get at the facts. King was horrified by the idea that labour and capital were in a struggle to the death. Workers and employers needed each other, King insisted, and both must remember that a third party was also involved—the public.

Mackenzie King had lots of chances to try out his ideas in the ten years after he joined the new department. Sent to British Columbia to end the violent 1902 railway strike, he was as angered by the radical labour leaders as he was by James Dunsmuir. These were not "reasonable men" like his friends Dan O'Donoghue or the plump Paddy Draper, the new secretary-treasurer of the Trades and Labour Congress. The strike, like so many others, ended in the disappearance of the union.

In 1906, King faced his toughest challenge. The United Mineworkers belonged to Gompers's American Federation of Labor, but it had some of the fire of the western unions. When the union organized Alberta coal mines, the mine owners refused to negotiate. The result was an eleven-month strike. Alberta coal kept prairie settlers warm during the long, harsh winters. By the autumn of 1906, the coal bins were empty and prairie people huddled down to face the coldest winter in memory. The young deputy minister of labour came to the rescue. In whirlwind negotiations that included a trip to union headquarters in Indianapolis, King forced a settlement. People, he insisted, could not be left to freeze.

Canadians had been shocked by the western coal blockade and horrified by violence at Buckingham, Quebec. The government must act. King was ready. There must be a law to make both sides wait while the public learned the facts. Then the side that continued the struggle unfairly would feel public anger. In 1907, Parliament gave Mackenzie King what he wanted: the Industrial Disputes Investigation (IDI) Act.

In a long career, King remembered his IDI Act with special pride. Although some of the ideas were borrowed from Australia and the United States, it was really King's invention. Since he believed that his heart was with the workers, he hoped that the Act would help them. Certainly workers who had a weak union now got a chance to state their case. However, union members soon found that the Act hurt them more than it hurt management. Since no strike or lockout was permitted during an investigation, employers could keep on operating. They could train workers to replace those who might go on strike. They could build up stock to supply their customers if a strike stopped production. Since public opinion was shaped by the wealthy men who owned newspapers, it seemed more likely to favour employers than workers.

There was one issue which Mackenzie King rarely considered when he was trying to end a dispute. Unions desperately needed to be *recognized* by employers. Otherwise, how could workers speak with a collective voice? Employers often refused to deal with a union. They hated the very idea of dealing with union representatives and officials whom they had not chosen themselves. Nothing in the IDI Act gave workers the right to join a union or compelled employers to negotiate if they did not want to do so.

At the time, criticism of the Act was drowned in a chorus of praise. King entered Parliament in 1908 and became Canada's first full-fledged Minister of Labour. All over North America he was recognized as an expert in the new field of industrial relations. When he was defeated in the 1911 election, King soon found a new career helping the powerful Rockefeller family in the United States with its labour problems. Instead of dealing with "unreasonable unions," King urged the Rockefellers to set up Employee Representation Plans so that workers and management could meet to discuss problems. Such plans became popular with many large American and Canadian companies in the 1920s. Oddly enough, Mackenzie King's idea came to be known as "the American Plan." Labour leaders condemned such plans as *company unions*.

In the years before the First World War, the IDI Act helped end many disputes but it could not stop a rising tide of labour protest. More and more workers showed that they would sacrifice almost anything for the right to choose their own union. One of the saddest and bitterest struggles was in the coal mines of Nova Scotia. After years of membership in the Provincial Workmen's Association, most miners wanted to join the United Mineworkers of America. The Dominion Coal Company refused to allow it. In 1909, miners on Cape Breton Island finally struck for the right to choose their own union. With help from the PWA, the company kept the mines open under military guard. For almost a year, miners and their families, evicted from company-owned houses, camped in tents on the bleak Cape Breton hills. At last they had to surrender. Three years later, when the United Mineworkers tried to organize Vancouver Island miners, the violence again brought soldiers to the coal fields. Hundreds of strikers were caged in barbed-wire concentration camps. The struggle lasted a year.

If unions could not defeat employers, could they win political battles? They tried. Between 1900 and 1914, Montreal, Winnipeg and Vancouver voters all sent labour members to the House of Commons in Ottawa. Other labour representatives won election to provincial assemblies and municipal councils. Yet, as Sam Gompers warned, politics split the workers. Men like Alphonse Verville, president of the Trades and Labour Congress and MP for Montreal-Maisonneuve from 1906 to 1921, had to work closely with the Liberals to have any influence. For that, they were seen as traitors to the unionists. Other union men, like Jimmy Simpson, columnist for the Toronto *Star* and a vice-president of the TLC, became socialists. Branches of the Socialist Party of Canada could be found from British Columbia to Cape Breton. Yet even the socialists were not united. Some of them agreed with Karl Marx, the great socialist thinker, that the revolution could come only after workers had been driven to the depths of misery. By working for better pay and working conditions, unions merely postponed the worker's paradise.

One radical organization treated politics and bargaining with equal contempt. The Industrial Workers of the World, an offshoot from the Western Federation of Miners, insisted that workers could have justice only when they forgot their differences, got together in a single organization and stopped work in a great general strike. The entire capitalist system would come to its knees. For the angry, powerless men in the bunkhouses of the Canadian and American West, this was an exciting message. Many thousands of them carried "Wobbly" cards or a copy of its famous little red songbook. In Edmonton and Victoria, when police arrested IWW speakers during their street-corner rallies, others took their place in a fight for free speech.

Some people still think that Canadians before the First World War lived in a golden age of innocence and happiness. In fact it was a

Members of the Western Federation of Miners parade in Cobalt in 1913. Unlike the more conservative craft unions, the WFM welcomed workers of every background and skill. It also urged radical political action.

time of harsh conflict. Canada was becoming a nation of city-dwellers, but it was hard to persuade people that old ideas would not work in a new setting. City councils were reluctant to provide parks, clean water and homes that working people could afford. Injured workers had to take their employer to court to get any compensation for medical expenses and loss of work. Not until 1914 did Ontario pass the country's first workmen's compensation act, guaranteeing medical care and a small pension for workers injured on the job.

By 1911, the Laurier boom was over. A new Conservative government under Robert Borden had to pick up the pieces. Thousands of unemployed workers flooded into the cities to look for work. The two new transcontinental railways skidded into bankruptcy. On the prairies, the crops failed for the first time since the 1890s. Finally, on August 4, 1914, Canada was at war.

The First World War

To the leaders of the Trades and Labour Congress, the war seemed like a plot by big business. Few Canadians took them seriously. Unemployment and patriotism persuaded thousands of young men to join the Canadian Expeditionary Force. Union members joined employers in calling for war contracts. Some unionists even insisted that workers from enemy countries should be locked up for the period of the war. By 1915, more than eight thousand recent immigrants were imprisoned in internment camps.

In 1914, few people expected a long war and no one predicted that Canada would soon face a desperate labour shortage. By 1916, with the government committed to putting half a million men in uniform, with munitions factories turning out shells and explosives, unemployment had vanished. The new Imperial Munitions Board had to dream up ways to get women to work in its factories. It even promised equal pay with men, an idea that seemed far more radical than giving women a vote in elections. Wages for almost everyone rose—but not as fast as prices. Sir Robert Borden's government did not want to interfere with business profits, nor would it raise taxes. Instead, it borrowed most of the money to pay for the war, a classic way to cause inflation.

In wartime Canada, union membership increased rapidly. Unions had always been active in metal manufacturing and they spread naturally into the new munitions factories. More surprising was the spread of unions in the civil service and even among police forces. That did not mean that employers had to bargain with their workers.

In Britain, munitions workers won the legal right to negotiate. In Canada, the British-controlled Imperial Munitions Board refused to follow the same rule. Its Canadian chairman, Sir Joseph Flavelle, felt that he had done enough merely by giving jobs to Canadian workers. In wartime, he could count on public opinion to condemn any strike as unpatriotic.

By 1917, many Canadian workers were angry enough to strike even in the face of the Industrial Disputes Investigation Act. Their leaders were angry that the Borden government had ignored them while British, American and French union leaders had been drawn into the national war effort. Conscription—a law that drafted men into the army—was the last straw.

Late in 1917 Sir Robert Borden had persuaded many Liberals to join his party in a Union government. Labour leaders made a hurried decision to fight the next election. On December 17, they were overwhelmingly defeated. Even working people wanted the new coalition to get on with winning the war. They were satisfied that Borden had finally chosen a labour unionist, Gideon Robertson of the Railway Telegraphers, as his new Minister of Labour.

The angry unionists in the West were not about to give up. No region of Canada had done more for the national war effort but none had a longer list of grievances against Ottawa. Farmers, workers, even a few businessmen, were thinking radical thoughts. Some union men had even turned back to the old Wobbly idea of general strike. In Winnipeg in the summer of 1918, city employees accidentally gave the idea a test. When members of other unions joined their strike, a committee of sympathetic citizens quickly patched up a settlement.

When the war ended on November 11, 1918, more Canadians belonged to unions than ever before. Leading unionists, however, were deeply divided. In the West workers were full of fight, but when the Trades and Labour Congress met at Quebec in the autumn of 1918, western delegates were outnumbered by cautious easterners. Wartime leaders were rejected. Like many other people in the postwar turmoil, the TLC leaders wanted to cling to the old principles of craft unionism.

The defeated but angry westerners decided to meet again at Calgary, in March 1919. Some of them had an ambitious plan. Instead of a planning session for the next TLC convention, the Calgary meeting became the starting point for a brand new labour organization, the "One Big Union." Unionists across western Canada would be asked to join an organization that scorned the old barriers of craft and which promised an exciting, if vague, new society for working people.

The Winnipeg General Strike

Plans for the One Big Union were still taking shape when one of its architects, Winnipeg's Bob Russell, discovered that his fellow unionists were determined to try another general strike. The stubborn men who owned Winnipeg's machine shops had refused to recognize Russell's local union of the International Association of Machinists. A general strike would quickly change their minds. Winnipeg's Trades and Labour Council asked its members. They agreed. At 11 A.M. on May 15, 1919, twenty-five to thirty thousand Winnipeggers walked out of their jobs to support the metal workers. More than half of them were not even union members!

Winnipeg was paralyzed. Its middle-class citizens were frightened. Russia and Germany were in the midst of revolution. Could it happen in Winnipeg? The strike committee was worried too. It told strikers to stay home or go to the park and enjoy themselves. It helped

Special constables are sworn in during the Winnipeg General Strike. A Citizens' Committee organized to fight the strike. When the city police was dismissed for sympathizing with the strikers, the Citizens' Committee provided replacements.

Roger Bray, a leader of the Winnipeg General Strike, speaks to strikers in Victoria Park. Strikers thought that city leaders would quickly agree to the union request for recognition. Instead, a Citizens' Committee of 100 organized swiftly to defeat the strike and punish its organizers.

to organize milk deliveries and told the police force—union members all—to stay on duty. For this the strike leaders were accused of trying to seize power. Returned soldiers, both for and against the strike, paraded the streets looking for excitement. As the first penniless workers began trickling back to their jobs, the federal government fired striking postmen. The city dismissed its unionized policemen and replaced them with men recruited by an anti-strike "Committee of One Thousand." The railway unions warned their members to go back to work or lose their pensions.

The Winnipeg General Strike would have been a disastrous defeat in any case, but the government took one more step. On June 17, before dawn, strike leaders were pulled from their beds and hurried to jail. On June 21, strikers and veterans thronged Winnipeg's Main Street in angry protest. The mayor called for troops and a contingent of Royal North West Mounted Police. When the crowd attacked a streetcar driven by a strike-breaker, the mounted police charged. Two men died and dozens were hurt. To Winnipeggers, it was "Bloody Saturday." Five days later, the Winnipeg General Strike was over. The angry men had been beaten.

Putting Up With It

Winnifred Wells looked quickly around. The forelady was at the far end of the long workroom. She leaned against the doorpost, easing her aching back. Tomorrow was her birthday, she thought, but there would be no celebration. With her mother and her unemployed brother to support, there was nothing left, and now even her wages had been cut.

"Miss Wells!" A man's voice broke her reverie. "Into my office!"

It was Mr. Jeffries, the new superintendent. Panic swept over her. At the end of the day, she could argue, a quality inspector never had anything to inspect. The seamstresses were too busy finishing their quotas. It was unfair to pester them. Winnifred started to explain.

"Miss Wells", Jeffries coldly interrupted, "Have you made up your time this week?"

Now Winnifred understood. A month before, the company had announced that inspectors would no longer earn a flat $15 a week. Instead they would get a cent and a quarter for each garment checked. Try as they could, Winnifred and the other inspectors could never make their old pay. In four weeks, Winnifred had never even earned the $12.50 minimum wage that the company was compelled to pay her.

"No," Winnifred admitted, "I guess I'm about forty or fifty cents short. But you know that the machinery broke down on Monday and then there was trouble with the collars on the new blouses . . ."

Jeffries stopped her with an angry gesture. "Miss Wells, you may go home now and do not return to work until I send for you."

Winnifred felt her heart stop. Without her meagre income, her family would have nothing. Anger battled with her terror at losing a job she had held for fourteen years. In desperation, she forgot her pride.

"Mr. Jeffries", she pleaded, "you know that I can't afford to leave now. I'm the only one bringing home an income in my family. Please sir, I'm sure I'll do better next week."

"Miss Wells, I am not obliged to explain company policy to you but as a favour, I shall do so. The law compels us to pay a minimum wage but it does not oblige us to keep employees who cannot earn it. Since Gavin's is a humane employer, we have decided, in view of your long service, to give you leave to recover your strength. At your own expense", he added.

"But how can I afford to live?" Winnifred cried.

"You must use your savings", Jeffries replied. "In these difficult times there are limits to what even the most generous employer can afford."

After six weeks, the Winnipeg General Strike had failed. So had similar strikes in Vancouver, Toronto and cities across the West. The government and wealthy citizens had been badly scared and now they wanted revenge. Ottawa cancelled the pensions of postmen who had joined the strike. Other workers were fired and some were blacklisted. For almost a year, trials of the strike leaders dragged on. Parliament had passed a law making it a serious crime to talk about overthrowing the government, and Winnipeg labour leaders were jailed for their angry speeches. Bob Russell, who had opposed the strike, got the longest sentence—two years.

The strike, and the hysteria with which it was crushed, hurt Winnipeg badly. The city stopped growing. People who might have started businesses or opened factories hesitated in the face of bad times. In spite of the bitterness, several strike leaders won seats in the Manitoba Legislature in 1920. One of them, John Queen, was later elected mayor of Winnipeg seven times. Bob Russell went on to a long career as a union leader and had a city high school named after him. Winnipeg's working class North End began a long tradition of electing labour and socialist members to Parliament. The first of them, in 1921, was James Shaver Woodsworth.

Labour Enters Politics

Woodsworth was a former Methodist minister and social worker who had lost his job during the war because he spoke out against fighting and killing. A frail, delicate man, he earned his living for a time as a dockworker in Vancouver. In 1919 he came home to Winnipeg on a

J. S. Woodsworth and other leaders of the young CCF meet with Jewish-Canadian labour leaders north of Toronto in 1936. Woodsworth's dream of a strong and democratic Canadian labour party would not come true in his lifetime.

lecture tour and helped to write the strikers' newspaper. He was jailed for what he wrote, some of it taken from the Bible, but he was soon released and the charges later were dropped. Woodsworth and another clergyman from Calgary, William Irvine, refused to join the established parties when they were elected. Instead, they formed a "Labour Group" in Parliament. Or, as Irvine explained, "Mr. Woodsworth is the leader and I am the group."

General strikes helped make 1919 the worst year for labour conflict in Canadian history. Most strikes failed but workers channelled their anger in a new direction. Not just in Winnipeg but across Canada, many working-men (and women too, since they could now vote) went to the polls to elect labour members. In Ontario and Alberta, farmer-labour governments won power, at least for a time. In Nova Scotia, a farmer-labour group formed the second largest party. Even in Ottawa, Woodsworth and Irvine found themselves, with sixty-five farmer-MPs, the second largest group in the House of Commons.

The strikes and the political strength of workers forced governments to look again at why working people were so angry. In Manitoba, a Royal Commission criticized radical union leaders but accused Winnipeg's business leaders of causing the strike by flaunting their wealth and by refusing to talk to their workers. A federal Royal Commission in industrial relations headed by Judge T.G. Mathers went much further. After listening to workers and businessmen from coast to coast, Mathers told Canadians that they had to face up to the problems of people who lived in cities and worked in factories. It was silly to pretend that people could still turn to their families in times of trouble or unemployment.

Over opposition from its business members, the Mathers Commission insisted that Canada must start insurance plans to protect workers from sickness, unemployment and the poverty of old age. Laws should set minimum wages, at least for women and children, and the eight-hour day should become standard. Unions should have the legal right to organize and bargain with employers.

The Mathers Commission forecast the kind of Canada we now know. If the recommendations had been adopted, much of the suffering of the following twenty years might have been avoided. In fact, many of the ideas were adopted by the Liberal party as part of its program to regain power. The Liberals also chose Mackenzie King as their new leader partly because they believed that he understood workers and their problems.

Unfortunately for workers, when King led his party to victory in 1921, he needed support from business and from farmers. Neither group believed in government programs to help workers, nor did they want to help unions. Even in the provinces where farmer and labour members tried to work together, there were deep differences. Since farmers worked long hours, so should workers. If workers earned higher wages, many things that farmers bought would cost more. When Ontario's farmer-labour government gave allowances to blind persons and to widowed mothers, its farm supporters protested at the cost. Labour voters were just as angry that the newly-elected governments did not do more. Across Canada, people seemed disillusioned with every kind of reformer, from those who had won votes for women to the people who had won prohibition of liquor in every province but Quebec.

Life in the   Roaring Twenties

For some Canadians, the postwar years meant an end to crusading for causes. The war had cost sixty thousand Canadian lives and an incredible amount of money. People were tired and they wanted to have fun. For some people, the next decade became the "Roaring Twenties." Unfortunately, most Canadians had no money to enjoy themselves. Their lives were as hard and narrow as ever.

We know a lot about how people lived in this period. The federal Department of Labour published statistics every month. Ministers, wondering why poor people had stopped coming to church, came to feel that they had to care for bodies before they could help the souls. Some, like Woodsworth and Irvine, decided that the churches belonged to the wealthy and angrily moved into labour and radical movements. A new profession of social work developed from the argument that charity had to be well organized. Social research became a small industry.

What people earned varied from town to town and from year to year. Beginning about 1908, prices in Canada began to rise very quickly. During the war years, the cost of living doubled. Wages followed more slowly. The old saying that "a dollar a day is very good pay" was soon forgotten. Experts who calculated what it should cost for food, rent, fuel, clothing and other basic needs claimed that a man who earned $13 a week in 1911 and $28 a week in 1921 could provide the basic necessities for the average family of five. Of course, many workers never earned that much and few worked a full fifty-two weeks a year. Most lost time from sickness or lay-off. Women received less than half a man's wage even when they did exactly the same work.

How did people manage? The simplest answer is that all members of the family worked, including mothers and children. Women who could not get a job took in boarders or did their neighbours' laundry. Children left school at fourteen—earlier if they could lie about their age. Very rarely did children in poor families go beyond Grade 8. Working people lived in horror of becoming dependent on charity. Neighbours helped each other, nursing the sick and even adopting children whose parents died, to save them from going to an orphanage. Most families lived on credit from the local grocery. A corner store that insisted on cash would soon have gone out of business. Paid holidays were a dream, but the few statutory holidays were enjoyed to the full.

Sometimes we assume that life has steadily improved. However, as far as we can measure the cost of living at that time, we know that the average Canadian worker could buy less in 1921 than in 1901. After that, wages rose a little faster than costs until about 1932, when conditions rapidly got worse. In 1929, before the Great Depression, the Department of Labour calculated that a family of four needed between $1200 and $1500 a year to buy the minimum comforts. It reported that sixty per cent of Canadian men and eighty per cent of Canadian women earned less than $1000 a year.

All was not bleak. While many businessmen opposed unions and reforms that could help working people, a growing number saw that happier employees could mean higher profits. They welcomed "scientific management." Tests showed that long hours led to accidents and poor workmanship. The eight-hour day became common, although many employees worked nine hours in order to have a half-day holiday on Saturday. Company pension plans spread. Wartime experience with factory lunchrooms had showed that well-fed workers produced more. The Mackenzie King idea of employee representation plans, popular in the United States, came home to Canada. Some provincial governments took up a British idea of "joint councils" with their civil servants. A few big companies, like Imperial Oil and the Dominion Foundry and Steel Company, set up joint councils and profit-sharing schemes which their workers still consider as a satisfactory substitute for unions. Businessmen could usually justify such reforms by pointing to higher profits and an absence of unions, but workers found that life on the job became pleasanter.

Governments, too, made lasting reforms. In 1927, thanks partly to J. S. Woodsworth's skilful tactics, Mackenzie King finally gave Canada an old-age pension law, though it was left to his Conservative successor, R. B. Bennett, to make it work. Most provinces adopted minimum wage laws for women and children. Ontario and the western provinces made secondary education available to all children. The war had shown Canadians how unhealthy many of them were. By the 1920s, city-dwellers were more likely to have clean drinking water and pasteurised milk. Tuberculosis, a widespread disease linked to bad living and working conditions, finally received serious attention.

If governments and employers improved the lot of working people, it was little thanks to unions. Canada's labour movement never experienced a more miserable decade. New unions and old suffered defeats. The International Association of Machinists, strong in the wartime munitions plants, almost vanished from Canadian factories. The veteran Typographers' Union held out for three years in a strike for the eight-hour day before giving up. During the war, union membership in Canada had doubled to 389,000. By 1924, it had tumbled to only 240,000.

The bitterest strikes of the 1920s were in the coal and steel industries of Cape Breton. By 1918, the United Mineworkers had finally been recognized by the mineowners, but the international union had no chance to enjoy the victory. A new corporation, British Empire Steel or BESCO, owned the island's steel mill and mines. A tough new manager, Roy Wolvin, cut wages and fired workers in a bid to make the industry profitable. First the steelworkers and then the miners struck. The Cape Breton miners ignored their union's firm rule against striking while a contract was in force. Their leader, J. B. McLachlan, was suspended by the union and jailed by the provincial government. From 1922 to 1926, the struggle continued. Mounted police attacked the strikers. Much of Canada's small army stood guard on the mines and mill. Across Canada, people collected food and clothing for Cape Breton strikers and their hungry wives and children. In the end, the workers lost, but so did Wolvin. He was fired as an embarrassment to the company.

In the Cape Breton strikes and across Canada, union men seemed to fight each other as much as they opposed employers. Until 1919, most unions in Canada had accepted the leadership of the Trades and Labour Congress. Now, that loyalty shattered. Across the Canadian West, thousands of union members voted to join Bob Russell's One Big Union. Within months, the OBU boasted thirty thousand members. Then it collapsed, almost as quickly as it had grown. When employers simply refused to negotiate with it, the international unions sent organizers to win back their former members. Most importantly, the OBU leaders could not agree on what to do next. By 1921, the One Big Union idea was dying, but it left bitterness and anger behind it.

The OBU had accused the international unions of being too conservative. In Quebec, a growing French-speaking and Catholic union movement accused the internationals of being too socialistic. As early as 1900, Catholic clergy in Quebec had tried to guide unions. They insisted that workers and their bosses were not enemies. Instead, they were partners, with different jobs to do. The Church would help settle their differences. Even in Quebec this idea made little impact until the First World War. Many French Canadians became very angry with English-speaking Canadians during the war years, particularly after conscription was enforced in 1917. People who had once been active socialists and union members now became Quebec nationalists. They worked with the clergy to create unions, or *syndicats*, which would shield Quebec workers from all the influences of North American life. In 1921 the Confederation of Catholic Workers was officially launched at Hull. By 1930 it had twenty-five thousand members.

Another split came in 1931 when the Trades and Labour Congress was forced to expel its largest affiliate, the Canadian Brotherhood of Railway Employees. In 1902, the TLC had made a rule that no national union could be a member of an international union organizing the same kind of workers. The Brotherhood of Railroad and Steamship Clerks (an international) insisted that the rule be kept. The president of the Canadian union, Aaron Mosher, was a formidable enemy. By 1926, he had collected most of the other purely Canadian unions into an All-Canadian Congress of Labour and launched an angry propaganda war against the TLC and its American-based affiliates.

Communism in Canada

The final threat to labour unity was the most dangerous. In 1917, the Russian Revolution had begun. A long, deadly civil war followed, and finally the Bolsheviks, under Vladimir Lenin, Leon Trotsky and Joseph Stalin triumphed. Was this really the beginning of the socialist revolution that Karl Marx had predicted? J. S. Woodsworth and many other socialists insisted that the Bolsheviks were enemies of socialism, kept in power by mass murder and terror. Still others believed just as passionately that Lenin had created the "dictatorship of the proletariat" Marx had predicted. Socialists everywhere, they insisted, must do all in their power, by fair means or foul, to help the Russian revolution. In 1921, in a barn near Guelph, Ontario, a few of the latter group founded the Communist Party of Canada.

Most of the Canadian Communists were active in unions, but their first loyalty was to the Communist International. Bob Russell learned his lesson early, when Moscow ordered all Canadian Communists to capture control of the Trades and Labour Congress by "boring from within." Russell was ordered to disband his creation, the One Big Union. He refused and was bitterly denounced. So were other Communists who did not obey orders. Moscow's strategy changed often and Communist leaders like Tim Buck and Tom Ewen learned to change their arguments overnight. In 1927, for example, the Communist International ordered its Canadian members to abandon "boring from within" and start their own organization, the Workers' Unity League.

Women stand guard at Flin Flon during the 1934 miners strike. Local merchants organized a back-to-work vote at the local community hall. The union asked miners' wives to guard the entrance because police would not want to fight them.

The Catholic, Communist and national labour organizations were not strong—each had about twenty-five thousand members—but the bitter fighting left no energy to organize new members. In Toronto and Montreal, strong unions among clothing workers were wrecked by Communist efforts to seize control. In Quebec, employers learned that Catholic unions sometimes became quite reasonable in their demands after a chat with their chaplains. As for the Trades and Labour Congress, its leaders grew steadily more cautious and pleased with themselves. A secret donation of $50,000 from a group of businessmen put the organization's finances on an even keel. It was easy enough to label critics as Communists and, indeed, many of them were. Because provincial and municipal governments tried to crush the Communists and their newspapers, many idealists saw them as martyrs. There was a steady trickle of recruits to replace those who were expelled or who left in disgust.

Canadian labour, with its quarrelling Catholic, Communist, national and international unions, was in a grim state by 1929. Though few people knew it at the time, so was the Canadian economy.

The Great Depression

In Canada, the Great Depression really began when the huge wheat harvest of 1928 could not be sold. Because they had no money, prairie farmers put off buying anything they could do without. So did the world-wide customers for Canadian lumber, paper and minerals. Canada was a world trader. Suddenly, nobody wanted what Canadians produced. For working people, the grim truth hit home in the spring of 1930. Winter was hard every year but people always found work when the warm weather returned. In 1930 they did not. Soon, savings were gone. Unemployment spread to the factories. By 1932, Montreal, Hamilton and Windsor had to support a third of their male workers. Railway workers, envied for their pensions and their security, faced wage-cuts and firing.

Depressions were nothing new. People remembered the 1913-14 depression or the 1907-08 period. In 1930, Canadian voters abandoned the Liberals to give Richard Bedford Bennett and the Conservatives a chance. In his booming voice, Bennett promised to blast a way into the markets of the world. The trouble was that the Depression got worse. By 1933, a quarter of all Canadians were hunting for work. A million and a half Canadians had been driven to the shame of relief. Even at the depth of the Depression, most people still believed that the unemployed should somehow have been able to help themselves. People who argued for unemployment insurance were accused of wanting to pay people for being lazy.

In the grim crisis, most Canadian unions felt that they could do little more than protect their own members. Except for construction workers, who suffered because there was almost no building, the craft unions of the Trades and Labour Congress survived the Depression with no more than wage cuts and a few losses. Of course, no one was eager to risk a strike or to spend money on organizing other workers. In 1932, when J. S. Woodsworth and the remnant of farmer and labour parties met at Calgary to form the Co-operative Commonwealth Federation (CCF), the TLC firmly rejected the new party. The TLC leaders preferred to use their influence with Liberal and Conservative politicians. Besides Aaron Mosher of the All-Canadian Congress of Labour had attended the Calgary meeting. Old rivalries mattered more than new ideas.

The one labour organization that fought back during the Depression was the Workers' Unity League. Communists believed that capitalism had met its hour of doom. WUL organizers were skilful, fearless and tireless. Many of them spoke Ukrainian and Finnish, the languages of many of the workers in mines and forests. Hungry, ill-paid coal miners at Estevan, women garment workers in Montreal, furniture workers and chicken pluckers at Stratford, lumber workers at Blubber Bay in British Columbia, all became part of the Communist struggle to organize unions at a time when desperate people would take any job. In the cities, Communists and sometimes supporters of the new CCF, organized "Unemployed Associations" to help people thrown out of their homes because they could not pay their rent. Bennett had established relief camps where single unemployed men could work for a wage of twenty cents a day. Communists organized a Relief Camp Workers Union to help the men protest the harsh military-style discipline in the camps.

For all their efforts, most of the Communist organizing endeavours failed, often with bloodshed. In 1930, two WUL organizers were found beaten to death near Thunder Bay. At Estevan, where union organizers sent miners and their families to fight the police, three miners died. Canadian governments might be helpless against the Depression but they were eager to fight the Communists. In 1931, the Ontario government arrested Communist leaders and, after a trial, most of them were sent to jail for long terms. Prime Minister Bennett promised to crush Communists "with the iron heel of ruthlessness." Some Canadians were shocked at the attack on civil liberties. A few joined the Communist party because the government had made men like Tim Buck into martyrs. Probably most Canadians agreed with the government. In times of trouble and uncertainty, people stick to old-fashioned ways.

In the spring of 1935, the Communists organized an "On-to-Ottawa" trek for unemployed workers. A thousand men travelled on boxcars as far as Regina. The leaders went to Ottawa, met Bennett and exchanged insults. On July 1, police and unemployed waged a pitched battle on Regina's market square. Public opinion was shocked by the harsh treatment of the unemployed, but the benefit went not to the Communists but to Mackenzie King. That September, the Liberals swept back to power with the slogan "King or Chaos."

There were other dramatic events in 1935. In Moscow, Stalin had become alarmed by the rise of Adolf Hitler in Germany. Orders went out to Communists in Canada to dissolve the Workers' Unity League and to join other unions to make a "Popular Front" against fascism.

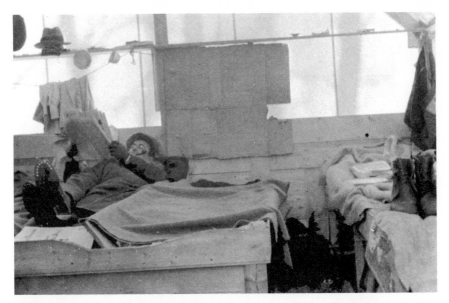

A bunkhouse for single unemployed men in Alberta in 1933. The Bennett government organized relief camps for the armies of jobless men who drifted across Canada during the 1930s. Conditions were primitive and the pay was only 20 cents a day.

The Americans Lead the Way

In the United States, President Franklin Delano Roosevelt had amazed Americans by tackling the Depression head-on. One answer, he believed, was to put more money in the hands of the workers. For the first time, an American president urged workers to join unions. In 1935, the Wagner Act was adopted. American unions could now force employers to bargain with them. A National Labour Relations Board would issue certificates to unions once workers had voted in favour of joining. They could punish employers who tried to frighten their workers away from joining. At last American union organizers could bring unions to workers in the huge factories and mills of the United States. Like the Knights of Labor sixty years before, new unions ignored the distinctions of trade and craft. Every worker in the plant, skilled or unskilled, would join the same union.

Industrial organizing swept into the steel mills and the rubber, glass and automobile factories of the northeastern United States. At the head of the movement was John L. Lewis, a huge, bushy-browed leader of the United Mineworkers, but the heroes of the movement

Women march during the 1937 autoworkers strike at Oshawa. The strike was one of the most important in Canadian history because it was the first victory in the long campaign to organize manufacturing workers.

were hundreds of tough young men and women, many of them socialists and Communists. The conservative craft unionists of the American Federation of Labor grew more and more angry. In 1937 came an open split. The industrial unions were expelled. At once they formed a Congress of Industrial Organizations. Its initials, CIO, became a magic symbol to workers in the United States and Canada.

In the 1930s, the spread of radios to almost every Canadian home linked people more closely to events in the United States. Canadians envied Americans their popular, energetic president. Roosevelt's "New Deal" let people know that someone was fighting the Depression. Now Canadian workers followed the exciting struggles of the CIO and its incredible victories in the huge industrial plants at Akron, Flint and Pittsburgh. In 1936, workers in a foundry at Point Edward, near Sarnia, Ontario, decided to imitate the CIO's successful sit-down strike tactics. In the winter of 1937, workers at the big General Motors factory at Oshawa signed up with the new United Auto Workers and demanded a contract. After all, the company had already signed an agreement with the union in the United States.

Canadians got some rude shocks. At Point Edward, vigilantes drove the strikers from the foundry, beating them with iron bars. Police arrested the battered strikers. Ontario's Liberal premier, Mitchell F. Hepburn, had been elected in 1934 as a friend of the workers, but he praised those who resisted the CIO. When the workers at Oshawa asked for a contract, it was Premier Hepburn who urged the General Motors management to refuse to negotiate. Hepburn believed that the CIO was a Communist conspiracy, bent on crippling Ontario's mining industry.

The CIO had more than it could do in the United States. When the Oshawa workers went on strike to win recognition of their union, the CIO's magic consisted of brave words and bluff. Hepburn claimed that there would be violence. He even recruited students as a special police force. The strikers christened them the "Sons of Mitches." The strike leader, Charles Millard, worked closely with Oshawa's mayor and police force. Despite Hepburn's warnings, the strike was peaceful. Finally, General Motors had had enough. Its American plants had a union, hard times seemed to be over by 1937, and the company reached a compromise settlement. It would negotiate with the union provided it did not call itself part of the United Auto Workers.

The CIO influence spread beyond Ontario. In Cape Breton, a tough Newfoundlander, Silby Barrett, painfully rebuilt the United Mineworkers. Money from the Nova Scotia workers actually helped the American CIO when its own funds had run out. In Alberta, packing plant workers tried the sit-down strategy, protesting terrible working conditions. Meat packers worked amid clouds of steam, blood, dust and dangerous chemicals. There was no violence at Edmonton and Calgary, but the strikers were defeated and many of them were blacklisted. Newspapers refused to report the disgusting conditions in the plants. Instead, they condemned the strikers as "foreign-born" troublemakers.

Without a law, unions could not organize factory workers. Few Canadians showed much desire to help unions. Soon after the Oshawa strike, Mitchell Hepburn called an election on his handling of the CIO. Ontario voters gave him a landslide victory.

During the strike, one of Hepburn's cabinet ministers, David Croll, had resigned in protest. "I would rather walk with the workers," he announced, "than ride with General Motors." After twenty years of prosperity and depression, most Canadians still preferred to ride with the company. It was safer.

Getting Organized

Tony Antonides raced across the street to the phone booth. The nickel almost slipped through his sweating fingers as he dropped it in the slot. He dialled and waited nervously. A second and then a third ring. Maybe they'd gone home. It was after midnight.

"Local Ten-oh-five, United Steelworkers," The voice sounded tired.

"It's Tony, down at the level crossing. They've got steam up on the engine and they're coming out to get the refrigerator cars. I've only got three guys here to stop them."

"Hang on Tony", the man answered. "Jake's on his way."

Tony went back into the hot night. Street lights left glistening reflections on the black water of Hamilton harbour. He looked over at the dark, familiar shape of the Stelco buildings. Two railway cars, with food for men still camped inside the plant, stood parked on the track across the road from the Stelco lot. CNR trainmen, with a friendly wave at the picketing steelworkers, had dropped them there that morning. Now, late at night, the company would collect them.

In the silence, he heard the puffing steam as the company locomotive started up. A group of men moved out on foot to clear the way. "Scabs," Tony growled, jaw hardening at the ugly, unfamiliar word. His brother-in-law would probably be among them. Tony picked up a stone, wondering if he could bring himself to throw it. If the company got the food, it would be one more victory.

The engine was almost up to the big gate now. The other pickets looked at him, silently seeking a lead. Wasn't anyone coming? Tony walked alone over to the level crossing. Suddenly, he saw the lights of a car. As it pulled up under the streetlight, he saw that it was Jake Hollister's ancient Hudson, almost buried under men. Jake ran over.

"They're coming out. Let's get a line across the tracks!" Jake grinned. "Okay, guys, they'll have to come through us. But no rough stuff. Put it down!" he shouted at a man who had picked up a length of pipe.

A hundred yards away, men from the plant had also lined up. Tony saw that most of them carried new baseball bats, shining white in the gloom. Maybe this was the time when the strike would get nasty. He also heard cars pulling into the street. Was it police? He knew the Hamilton force would be neutral. The mayor, old Sam Lawrence, had promised that. Maybe these were provincial police. Tony could not bear to look. He stood waiting, listening.

Behind him, there was a crunch of gravel and the sound of heavy breathing. Finally, Tony forced himself to look. From who knows where, hundreds of pickets had arrived. They stood now, silently waiting. Suddenly, there were shouts and a swelling chorus of cheers.

At the gate, the locomotive, wheels grinding, backed away. The men with the baseball bats slowly turned and followed. The picket line had held.

The Second World War

On September 10, 1939, Canada declared war on Hitler's Germany. There was none of the excitement of 1914. Few people any longer believed that war was romance.

As in 1914, war helped lift Canada out of a deep depression. In 1939, a million Canadians still collected relief money. By the time C. D. Howe, the Minister of Munitions, returned from England in 1940, the government knew that any war material Canadian factories could produce, from warships to radar sets, from bombers to binoculars, would be needed. By 1941, Canada was so short of people for her factories and armed forces that every man and woman was forced to register and to go to whatever job the government wanted done.

Mackenzie King wanted to avoid the mistakes Sir Robert Borden had made in the earlier war. Instead of borrowing money, the government collected taxes to pay for the war effort. When prices soared in 1940-41, a Wartime Prices and Trade Board tried to freeze the cost of living. It largely succeeded. A National War Labour Board ordered that wages be kept at no more than 1925-29 levels, with a cost-of-living bonus if prices rose higher. By 1942, an employee could not quit a job or be fired without government permission. Able-bodied men were

Unions did more than wage strikes and demand higher pay. Unions like the Halifax Longshoremen's Association made sure that jobs were given out fairly to their members, helped out in times of sickness or unemployment, spoke up for members who felt unfairly treated and sometimes provided retirement benefits.

switched from jobs the government said were unimportant. In a few short years, King's government was running the whole Canadian economy. There were mistakes and complaints, of course, but many ordinary Canadians had never been better off.

Canada's unions were as divided about the war as they had been about the Depression. The war should have pleased the Communists. Since 1936, they had urged Canada to fight Hitler. In 1937, Communists had helped send more than a thousand young Canadians to fight fascism in Spain. Suddenly, on the eve of war in 1939, Russia signed a friendship pact with Hitler. Overnight, Canadian Communists were ordered to change their minds. Scattered in key positions in many unions, the Communists were ordered to support Russia's new policy by strikes and other actions. By the summer of 1940, many Communists had been put in internment camps with Canadian Nazis; others fled to the United States. In Quebec, members of the Catholic unions were no more in favour of the war than other French Canadians but they would not break the law.

Divisions and Alliances

In 1939, Canadian labour had a new division and a new alliance. In the United States, the American Federation of Labor had driven out its CIO unions. Now it insisted that the Trades and Labour Congress do the same. Reluctantly, the TLC agreed. Very quickly, the CIO unions linked up with Aaron Mosher's shrinking national unions to form the Canadian Congress of Labour (CCL).

The war brought a scramble of union organization. Instead of just making artillery shells, Canadians turned out ships, airplanes, trucks, tanks, guns, radios and radar sets. Every kind of raw material, from steel and aluminum to synthetic rubber and uranium oxides, was needed for the war effort. When the industrial unions in the new CCL started organizing, the richer unions in the TLC joined in. The old craft principles were forgotten in the race to sign up workers in shipyards, factories and mills. By 1944, Canada had twice as many union members as in 1939. But the road was not smooth for union organizers.

C. D. Howe, the man in charge of wartime production, had no love for unions. He invited successful business leaders to join in running the wartime economy. These "dollar-a-year" men did not want unions to take advantage of the war to win members. In 1939, thanks to J. S. Woodsworth, Parliament had made it a crime to fire a worker just for supporting a union, but it took a stupid employer to fail to find some other reason to fire a pro-union person.

Mackenzie King had extended the Industrial Disputes Investigation Act to all war industries. In the winter of 1941-42, gold miners at Kirkland Lake found out how little help Mackenzie King's law actually gave them. Most miners had joined a union. The mining companies refused to recognize it. An investigation under the IDI Act, headed by Mr. Justice C. P. McTague, heard both sides and agreed with the miners. The companies paid no attention. The miners went on strike but after hungry months of waiting, they gave up. Many drifted away to join the army or to work in other industries.

Of course, not all employers fought unions. Many believed that unions were part of a modern industry. With business booming in wartime, even anti-union managers did not want to interrupt production because of a strike. Since the government tightly controlled wages and profits, there was not much that a union could do for its members during wartime. Once peace returned, many industries—and their unions—would obviously vanish. Meanwhile, some unions were almost helpful. In 1941, when Hitler attacked Russia, Canadian Communists switched sides again. They demanded a bigger Canadian war effort. Unions they controlled agreed not to strike while the war was on.

By 1943, no one doubted that Hitler would be beaten. After four years of war and ten years of Depression, many Canadian workers were fed up with low pay and long hours. Even in wartime, it was obvious that people with money could buy luxuries and have a good time. The pleasures did not reach most working Canadians. Their one big wartime gain was a system of unemployment insurance. It took effect in 1942, at a time when almost no one was out of work.

An Important Victory

Government rules prevented unions from striking for more money. Or did they? Silby Barrett, now head of the CIO in Canada, made Charles Millard the head of the Steelworkers' Organizing Committee. By 1942, Millard's union represented workers in two of the four biggest steel mills, at Sydney and at Sault Ste. Marie. He could not win the others if he did not show them that the union could raise their low wages.

First, Millard argued that steel was a vital national industry and a steelworker in Sydney or Montreal should earn as much as in Hamilton or the Soo. He had no trouble showing that the cost of living was the same or even higher where wages were lowest. Some industries would be national, the government agreed, but steel would not be one of them. Millard insisted that steelworkers must have a standard wage of fifty-five cents an hour. In January 1943 his members went on strike. The strike was illegal, but steel was vital to almost every war industry and no one else could do the steelworkers' hot, unpleasant work. C. D. Howe was furious but finally the government gave in.

There were many other strikes that year. Quebec Catholic unions organized the pulp and paper industry. In British Columbia, the International Woodworkers of America finally broke through the opposition of the forest companies. In Montreal, a city that had gone bankrupt during the Depression, civic workers had lived for years with miserable pay and long hours. One after the other, the garbage workers, the firemen, the police, even the city's tax collectors, went on strike for higher pay and the right to have a union. Like 1919, 1943 was a year of strikes and labour anger in most parts of Canada.

The Co-operative Commonwealth Federation

It was also the year of the Co-operative Commonwealth Federation, the party J. S. Woodsworth had founded in 1932. Most of the CCF's few supporters in the 1930s were prairie farmers. In union ranks, it was opposed by Communists and by Liberal and Conservative sympathisers. Few working people took it seriously. By 1940, the party seemed dead. Suddenly, to most people's surprise, its support grew. The war seemed to show that the CCF's ideas about planning and spending made sense. Why could so much be done to fight Hitler and so little to fight the Depression? CCF leaders like M. J. Coldwell and David Lewis gained an audience. Union leaders like Mosher and Millard backed the party, and in 1942, for the first time in history, a Canadian labour organization, the Canadian Congress of Labour, endorsed a political party. A year later, in July 1943, the CCF came within a few seats of forming the government in Ontario. It was already in second place in British Columbia and Manitoba. The party's biggest gains had come where union members had given their backing.

For Mackenzie King, the strikes and the victories of the CCF were a warning. If he did not do more for workers, his Liberal government might face the same disaster as Borden's government. Something had to be done.

One reason why people were poor was that they could not afford the cost of raising children. In 1942, Leonard Marsh, a professor, had suggested that the government pay a "family allowance" for each child in a family. At the time, King had snorted at the notion. Under the threat of workers voting for the CCF, he found the idea more interesting.

King also invited Judge Charles McTague to become chairman of the National War Labour Board. Although McTague was a Conservative, he had shown his understanding of labour in the Kirkland Lake fight. Soon, McTague reported to the prime minister. Too many strikes, he told King, were not about money or hours of work. They were about the right to organize a union. Canada needed a law like the Wagner Act in the United States. At first, King was angry. He thought his own IDI Act was the only law Canadian workers needed. More strikes and more signs of CCF strength changed his mind.

P.C. 1003 and the Rand Formula
In February 1944, Mackenzie King and his ministers approved P.C. 1003, the National War Labour Order. It put together both King's and McTague's ideas. A union that proved it had workers' backing could

get a certificate as bargaining agent. Employers would be forced to deal with such a union. Both companies and unions were forbidden from "unfair practices" that might stop workers from making a free choice. A board with representatives of business, labour and government would make sure the rules were obeyed. King's ideas about investigations, cooling-off periods and peaceful discussion were also part of the new order.

P.C. 1003 is the most important labour law in Canadian history. By 1948, it had become a real law, approved by Parliament. Provinces also adopted it and changed it to suit their taste. The basic idea remains that governments will help workers to make a free choice of whether or not to have a union. Just as important is the idea that a legal strike cannot happen until a contract between a company and a union has run out. Even then, governments have a right to get both sides to try to settle a dispute without a strike or a lockout.

Unions needed something more if they were to work for their members: money. A union might have a certificate but it would be powerless if workers would not share the costs. Many of the new unions barely existed because members did not pay their dues and employers refused to help. In the fall of 1945, the United Auto Workers called a strike at the Ford Motor Company in Windsor. Their main demand was that the company deduct union dues from each worker's pay cheque. The company refused, though its American parent had such an agreement.

The Ford strike was long and sometimes bitter. At one point, strikers blocked traffic in front of the plant and filled an entire street with cars. The government threatened to send soldiers. The union called for a general strike. In the end, the argument was settled by Judge Ivan C. Rand. He scolded the union for its car blockade and other illegal tactics, but he agreed that every worker in a plant benefits from a union. Some workers might have personal or religious reasons for not wanting to join a union, but it was only fair that they pay their share of the costs and that the company collect the money and hand it over to the union. The "Rand Formula" became a Canadian answer to the problem of union security.

Together, P.C. 1003 and the Rand Formula gave Canadian unions a strength they had never had before. As the war ended, it seemed that they would need all the power they could have. Most Canadians feared that the Depression would return with the peace. Once again, Mackenzie King remembered that postwar misery as much as wartime mistakes had hurt the Borden government. He asked C. D. Howe to organize the postwar period as he had managed Canada in wartime. Most businessmen were happy to co-operate. They trusted Howe. Many of them now realized that family allowances and unemployment insurance helped them as much as poorer Canadians. Only when people spend money can companies make profits.

King's efforts paid off. In the 1945 election, Canadians gave the Liberals a narrow majority. Union members who had voted CCF in 1943 switched back to the Liberals. For the first time in its history, the Trades and Labour Congress urged members to back a political party—the Liberals. So did the Communists. The CCF, which had seemed on the verge of victory two years before, was shattered.

Canada After the War

Postwar Canada had many problems. There was a shortage of homes, cars, refrigerators, even kitchen tables and cribs. Manufacturers

The postwar period saw more strikes in Canada than at any time since 1919. Public opinion blamed unions. This restaurant owner was angry that Montreal bus drivers walked out for shorter hours and better pay, disrupting service.

The car blockade during the 1945 strike at the Ford Motor Company in Windsor. To prevent cars and workers from entering or leaving the plant, strikers simply drove past the plant, stopped their cars, locked the doors and went home. The most important result of the strike was the Rand Formula.

found that they could sell anything they produced. Prices, held down for most of the war, began to rise. Union members demanded that their leaders do something.

Unions in the Canadian Congress of Labour planned a single national campaign for 1946, with members demanding a forty-hour week, two weeks annual vacation with pay, and a raise of nineteen and a half cents an hour. Beginning with the woodworkers in British Columbia and sweeping through textile workers, rubber workers, electrical workers and steelworkers, the industrial unions made 1946 rank with 1919 and 1976 as among the biggest years for strikes in Canadian history.

The most dramatic strike in 1946 happened at the Steel Company of Canada plant in Hamilton. Charles Millard's United Steelworkers had won only a narrow victory among the Stelco workers, who were among the best paid in the industry. Would a strike succeed in a plant where almost half the eight thousand workers had refused to join the union? To make matters worse, the Steelworkers would have to fight the government. Humphrey Mitchell, the Minister of Labour, had declared that workers could have a raise of no more than ten cents an hour. If there was a strike, the government warned, the union would be breaking the law. "If they arrest five on the strike committee," answered a union official, "five more will take their place."

On July 15, the strike began. Elsewhere, steel mills shut down and picketing was routine. At Stelco, the company brought in a thousand workers, hired airplanes and boats to bring in food and supplies, and promised to break the strike. Outside, Local 1005 of the Steelworkers blocked the streets and, to its own amazement, found that most of the city supported it. The government sent police to break through the throngs of picketers, thought about public opinion, and pulled back. In the end, the strike was settled in a compromise.

Most strikes ended that way in 1946, but sometimes, there were cruel defeats. In Cape Breton, where a quarter of the men were out of work after the war, miners waged a last, hopeless strike in 1947. Printers in Winnipeg lost their jobs. So did textile workers at Valleyfield in Quebec. Strikes grew longer because unions and their members

Striking Montreal bartenders had to insist that their strike was legal. Under the Duplessis government, Quebec labour legislation was a serious barrier to unions seeking to protect their members. One unhappy outcome was that many unions had to bend or break the law to survive.

were harder to starve into submission. However, both sides also learned to compromise. The long strikes of 1946 and 1947 often led to years of labour peace. Each side had tested the other's strength.

Whether union leaders were Communists, CCF supporters or non-partisan, there was not much difference in the way they did their job. There was a growing difference in the way they saw each other. From the 1930s CCF-ers and Communists had fought each other for control of industrial unions. CCF supporters believed that Communists had helped destroy their chances in 1945. In the 1946 strikes, Millard was determined that his Steelworkers would do as well as the Communist-run unions. After 1946, the fight was in the open in the Canadian Congress of Labour. Millard of the Steelworkers and Pat Conroy, the CCL secretary fought the Communists and drove them or their unions out of the organization.

The rival Trades and Labour Congress moved more slowly. For one thing, its secretary-treasurer, Pat Sullivan, was a Communist. In 1947 he quit the party and reported that the Communists had ordered his Canadian Seamen's Union into costly, unsuccessful strikes because of Russian needs. Sullivan's claims and American pressure forced the TLC to act. With help from the Liberal government, another union, the Seafarers' International Union, came to Canada. Using violent and sometimes illegal methods, its leader, Hal Banks, drove the Canadian Seamen's Union out of existence.

By 1950, most Communist influence was gone from both the big labour organizations. Some Communist-led unions like the United Electrical Workers held on to their members and rejoined the Canadian Labour Congress in 1972. Others broke up or joined unions like the United Steelworkers.

Into the Fifties

Canada in 1950 looked very different from the Canada of 1939. One big change was seen in the 1951 census. In the 1921, 1931, and 1941 censuses, more than two-thirds of Canadians had been so poor that they could not afford even a barely decent life. Dramatically, in 1951, the "poor" had been cut to a third of all Canadians. It was still far too many, but what had happened in ten years to make a difference? There are many answers, but the growth of unions and their influence on the wages of workers who did not even belong to unions must be part of the explanation.

Yet, if there was a change between 1941 and 1951, it stopped hap-

Striking asbestos workers march to mass in 1949. The historic strike at Asbestos pitted Catholic workers against a powerful American corporation. Church leaders like Archbishop Joseph Charbonneau supported the strikers. The provincial government of Maurice Duplessis backed the company.

pening. In 1961 and 1971, a third of Canadians were still poor. Perhaps by coincidence, unions stopped growing.

Unions themselves began to worry about their failure to grow. Too much energy was wasted when unions in the rival congresses fought each other. Many of the old differences were gone. Organization drives during the war had ignored old distinctions between "craft" and "industrial" unions. By now, international unions dominated both the TLC and the CCL. Both agreed that Canada must support the western democracies against aggression from the Soviet Union. Both called for a united Canadian labour movement.

The Asbestos Strike
Indeed, by the 1950s, reunion could include Quebec's Catholic unions.

Ten years before, that had been impossible. Other unions remembered how an archbishop had ended a strike at Valleyfield by ordering women to go back to work for less than Quebec's minimum wage. There were angry stories of priests making deals with employers in return for a donation to the Church. The war years had changed all unions, including those in Quebec. New leaders like Gerard Picard and Jean Marchand respected the Church but acted like union organizers. Quebec's postwar government, under Maurice Duplessis, began treating all unions as enemies. Businessmen complained that Quebec workers now wanted the same wages and rights as other Canadians.

The break came in 1949, at Asbestos, when a Catholic union ignored some of the steps Quebec law demanded before workers could strike. Backed by their chaplain, led by Jean Marchand, the asbestos miners went on strike. Duplessis was furious. Squads of provincial police invaded the little mining town. Strikers were taken to hotel basements and beaten while reporters looked on. Quebec was deeply divided. Archbishop Joseph Charbonneau supported the strikers. Other bishops backed the government. Pierre Elliott Trudeau, then a law professor in Montreal, claimed that the Asbestos strike helped make modern Quebec. For a time, it also brought all Canadian workers together.

Getting together seemed the only way to add more union members in Canada. The Canadian Congress of Labour, with 350,000 members, wasted money trying to attract some of the Trades and Labour Congress's 522,000 members. If both congresses joined with the Catholic unions, more than a million workers would belong to one organization. Merger became possible in 1953 when the two American central organizations, the AFL and the CIO, agreed to get together. By the summer of 1956, the Canadian merger was complete. The Canadian Labour Congress (CLC) had been created.

A New Political Party

Only one argument had threatened to split the two Canadian congresses: what to do about politics? A survey showed that most Canadian union leaders now voted for the CCF, but many would not. In 1958, the Canadian Labour Congress reached its decision. It would work with the CCF to start a new party, bringing back people who had given up on the older organization. At Ottawa in 1961, two thousand people met to launch the New Democratic Party (NDP). The CLC slipped into the background. It would support the new party, but it

Delegates at the Founding Convention of the New Democratic Party cheer the election of Tommy Douglas as leader of Canada's first real labour-backed party. Unlike Canadian unions, American labour organizations have never tried to establish their own political party.

still had to work with the Conservative and Liberal politicians who formed governments.

Few Canadian workers shared the worries that led union leaders into mergers or into founding a more powerful labour party. By 1956, the average industrial wage, $62.40 a week, had doubled since 1945 and tripled since 1939. The average family had twice the spending power it would have had during Depression days. Many could buy one of the flickering new black-and-white television sets and make the down-payment on a home or even a cottage by a lake.

There were exceptions. There was not much wealth in Cape Breton or in Canada's newest province, Newfoundland. Families could be crushed by huge hospital and doctors' bills. Many companies now had pension plans and workers could retire at sixty-five or seventy, but if the company went out of business, the worker could lose everything. Employers were not obliged to pay women as much as men, even for the same work. Still, more and more Canadians took a forty-hour week for granted. Getting extra money for working overtime was no longer an oddity. Things were better.

Though few Canadians realized it, Canada had ten years after 1945 before war-devastated countries like Germany, Japan or Italy could climb back as competitors. Canadians might have used the time to build a permanent lead, but little money was spent training skilled workers or designing new factories. By 1957, unemployment began to rise. Manufacturers found it harder to sell Canadian goods. People blamed unions for making Canadian workers too well paid. Instead of launching a new drive to add members, the Canadian Labour Congress and its members were forced to fight for what they had.

In Newfoundland, the Liberal government of Joey Smallwood did everything it could to prevent the International Woodworkers of America from organizing the island's loggers. When one of the two big logging companies took on the union, Smallwood announced that he would "free the loggers of Newfoundland from a foreign union." He outlawed the union at a special session of the provincial legislature. In the violence that followed, a policeman died and dozens of strikers were arrested. Unions across Canada collected $856,000 for the Newfoundland loggers but most people on the island believed in Premier Smallwood.

Having driven out the International Woodworkers, Smallwood invited another union, the United Brotherhood of Carpenters and Joiners, to take over. This was one of the biggest and most conservative unions in North America. The Canadian Labour Congress could do little about it.

Still, unions in Canada had come a long way since 1939. Editors and politicians already liked to say that "Big Labour" and "Big Business" were equal in power. However, one labour leader, listing Canadian labour's defeats in the 1950s, put it differently:

"Sure they're the same—big mountain and big molehill."

Trouble and Strife

Chapter **6**

Roland Cormier left the old couple in his motel room and headed for his car. They would be there when he got back, waiting for the news. Most likely it would be bad.

Butch Arsenault had a drinking problem. After three warnings, he had been fired. Twice the union had gone to bat for him. Not now. Five years before, Cormier remembered, Arsenault had been president of the local. Then he had been voted out by younger members who claimed they could get a better contract. What was more, they were right. After a short strike, the union had won the best contract in the district. Butch Arsenault, beaten and disgraced, had begun drinking heavily.

"We warned him", the local president told Cormier. "We've spent a couple of thousand dollars getting his job back. The members won't put up the money any more."

Roland Cormier could understand. Before he became a full-time representative for the union, he too had been a union president. He had won the job from an older man like Butch Arsenault. Yet, without people like Butch, would there ever have been a union at all? It had taken courage back in the fifties to start a union in a small Nova Scotia town. The union owed Butch one more try—especially if Butch and his wife were serious about their part of the bargain.

Cormier slid his car into a visitor's parking space beside McArdle Manufacturing and went into the office. Bill McArdle met him.

"Can I get you a coffee, Rolly?" McArdle began, when they had sat down in the inside office. "I guess you're here about Arsenault." Cormier agreed.

"Sorry, Rolly, but he's had his last chance. We can't have a drunk working with machinery. Our safety record would be shot. You

know as well as I do that the local union won't back him this time. I'll even do something about his pension though officially he's got nothing coming to him."

"Look, Bill," Cormier began, "Butch Arsenault had eighteen years here. For thirteen of those years, he was the best machinist in the plant. Your dad could tell you that. He also tried to run the union in a way that was good for the company as well as the members. Maybe that was his mistake. Some of the present officers still haven't forgiven him. Butch has had a pretty lonely time in this plant.

McArdle was silent but his face had softened a little.

"I'm not asking for his reinstatement now", Cormier continued. "I've talked to Butch and his wife. They're a pretty strong couple. This morning, I pulled a few strings to get Butch into a treatment program at Halifax. His wife is sticking by him. What I'm asking from you, Bill, is a promise to keep Butch's job open if he pulls himself together within the next three months. He needs that kind of encouragement."

McArdle thought for a moment and smiled.

"Rolly, you get me back the old Butch Arsenault and we're all winners. If we can't do that, we're all losers. You've got a deal."

Labour in Canada seems to go through ups and downs. The 1960s and 1970s saw both. People earned incomes which their parents could never have imagined. They also had to meet costs that seemed to rise as fast as their wages. Women began to make some headway in their fight for equal wages and opportunities for promotion, but unemployment for men and women stubbornly increased, especially for the young and unskilled. Civil servants, teachers, even some police and firefighters, won the right to strike. Their employers—the public— soon became as angry as any manufacturer at the cost of wage settlements and the inconvenience of strikes.

Labour in the Sixties

By 1960, some of the hopes born with the new Canadian Labour Congress had died. Quebec's Catholic unions did not join. Instead, under Jean Marchand, they cut their ties with the Church to become the Confederation of National Trade Unions (CNTU). It was one of the first signs of Quebec's "Quiet Revolution" of the 1960s. The CLC's political hopes were also disappointed. The New Democratic Party won only a foothold in Parliament; most union members voted

Union leaders debate policy with members during a meeting of Local 6500, United Steelworkers, in Sudbury. Unions with a powerful social conscience like the Steelworkers had to make sure their concerns were widely shared by thousands of members across Canada.

Liberal or Conservative. Although business supported the two older parties, many Canadians did not think it right that unions should back a party of their own. In British Columbia, where the NDP was strongest, the government banned unions from making political contributions.

Canadian unions had always been proud of their honesty. There was one ugly exception. In 1949, the government had encouraged Hal Banks, an ex-convict, to come to Canada to fight a Communist-run seamen's union. Banks used his violent and dishonest methods against all unions in Great Lakes shipping, but only in 1960 did the CLC expel him and his Seafarers' International Union. A government investigation found seventy-five cases of violence by Banks and his henchmen. Cleaning up the problem was all the harder because Banks's union had the support of President John F. Kennedy of the United States.

Political defeats and corruption were national events. The real story of labour is usually local and barely heard. Unions had helped change the lives of millions of Canadians since the Second World War,

Violence during a strike by the Teamsters' union in Quebec. While the law allowed strikers to inform the public that a dispute was in progress, angry workers sometimes attacked strikebreakers, forcing police to intervene.

but now they were under attack. Employers had learned to meet union demands with a list of their own proposals. Bargaining became a skilled profession with company experts matching union statistics. The law now forced employers to deal with a properly certified union, but a company was not forced to negotiate quickly. If signing a first contract was delayed for a few years, employees got tired of paying union dues and gave up. In some provinces, winning recognition for a union became harder. Governments wanted to make sure that the individual's right *not* to belong to a union was protected.

A century before, unions had grown up to protect skilled workers like shoemakers and coopers (barrel-makers) from losing their jobs. New machines and changing needs were now wiping out entire occupations. In the 1950s, two strikes by the Brotherhood of Locomotive Firemen could not change the fact that diesel engines ran on oil, not coal. Firemen were no longer needed. In 1964, members of one of Canada's oldest unions, the Toronto printers, went on strike because their jobs were threatened by new machinery. They lost. Everywhere, workers feared that automation would replace people with machines leaving them no way to earn a living.

Most labour leaders realized that it was hopeless to fight change. The fair answer was to make sure that workers shared the gains as well as the costs of change. Sensible employers agreed. Others ignored workers, making changes which cost employees hard-won contract gains. In 1965, when the Canadian National Railways used new engines to bypass long-established stopping places, some workers went on strike. After an investigation, Mr. Justice Samuel Freedman scolded the men for breaking the law, but he also said that unions must have the right to bargain about new machinery that changed jobs or even wiped them out altogether.

Perhaps the biggest labour problem facing many governments across Canada in the 1960s was what to do about their own employees. Civil servants had always accepted low pay in return for a pension and steady work. Now unionized workers had won better benefits and similar security. Meanwhile, because of Canada's economic problems in the late 1950s, promised pay raises for federal civil servants had been delayed again and again. By 1963, the Liberals and Conservatives had joined the New Democrats in promising unhappy federal workers that they would be allowed to bargain and even to go on strike.

The idea was not completely new. Postal workers had formed a union as early as 1891, but they had no right to go on strike. When they did so in Winnipeg in 1919, many of them lost their jobs and their pensions. In 1944, when the CCF won power in Saskatchewan, it allowed its civil servants to form unions and to go on strike. Twenty years later, Quebec's provincial employees won the same right.

In the summer of 1966, postal workers got tired of waiting for better pay and walked out in an illegal strike. Many Canadians were shocked to learn how little letter carriers and mail sorters earned. A settlement came quickly.

The biggest concession was the Public Service Staff Relations Act, approved by Parliament in 1967. The PSSRA, with the IDI Act and PC 1003, were the three most important labour laws in Canada. Like other labour relations acts, the PSSRA made rules about how civil servants could choose unions to represent them. Workers in each of the new bargaining units could decide whether they wanted the right to strike or whether they would accept the decision of an arbitrator or judge in any disagreement over their contract. The government chose one of its departments, the Treasury Board, to act as employer in negotiating with its employees. Most civil service organizations joined to form the Public Service Alliance of Canada. It became Canada's third largest union.

Across Canada, most provincial governments followed Ottawa's example, although Alberta and Ontario refused to let their civil servants have the right to strike. The merger of the TLC and the CCL led to creation of the powerful Canadian Union of Public Employees (CUPE). By 1972, CUPE had become the largest union in Canada, bigger than the United Steelworkers.

The growth of the new public-sector unions increased the number of Canadians in unions. From 1956 to 1963, the unions' share of Canadian workers had fallen from thirty-three percent to twenty-eight percent. Now it rose again to over thirty-three percent. Newly organized workers expected gains. Strikes by government employees affected millions of people. A mail strike meant that no one got letters or bills. Without air traffic controllers, most planes were grounded. When city employees walked out, huge mounds of garbage collected.

Professionals like teachers, nurses and engineers also began to think about forming unions and seeking the right to strike. In the past, their associations and federations had opposed such tactics as "unprofessional" and unnecessary. Now it seemed that unions had won better incomes for less qualified workers and wiped out some of the advantages of being a professional. Public opinion was shocked when it saw teachers and nurses on a picket line. Governments found that they could collect taxes whether or not they provided full public services. Parents and students got more angry at striking teachers than at the politicians and officials who managed the schools.

In the 1960s, young people who could not remember the hard times of the Depression flocked into unions. Often they refused to accept agreements made by older, more cautious union leaders. This resulted in more strikes, some of them illegal or "wildcat." In 1966, Canada's railways were stopped by a strike for the first time in sixteen years. At Montreal, where preparations for Expo 67 were behind schedule, construction workers won record wages. Montreal dock workers closed the port until they got their share. Next, workers on the St. Lawrence Seaway warned that they would do the same. Under the threat, a government official agreed to a thirty percent wage increase. A storm of protest rose from people who feared that the Seaway settlement would set an example for all workers. Industrial relations in Canada seemed to be in a mess. Ottawa asked H. D. Woods, a re-

A demonstration during the Common Front strikes in Quebec in 1972. The provincial government decision to jail three union leaders for defying a court order angered many younger union members. The CSN is the Quebec-based Confederation of National Trade Unions.

spected expert from McGill University, to head a study of the whole system.

In the circumstances, Canadians were probably surprised when the Woods task force reported in 1969 that unions and management had made collective bargaining work fairly well. Any other system would only have encouraged more government interference.

The Uneasy Seventies

By the time Woods reported, Canada had a new prime minister. Pierre Elliott Trudeau had backed the Asbestos strikers in 1949, but union leaders found him hard to figure out. In 1968, the new prime minister announced that there would be no more "free stuff." In 1972, the Trudeau government turned unemployment insurance into a system that paid money to the old, the sick and to women who left work to have a baby. In 1974, Mr. Trudeau attacked the idea of wage and price controls. In 1975, he put controls into effect.

One Trudeau idea did not change. He did not agree with na-

Ontario teachers protest against laws that would have banned their right to strike. Like other professionals and public employees during the 1970s, teachers found that they shared many of the social and economic concerns of other workers.

tionalism in Canada or in his native Quebec. Many Canadians felt differently. They had welcomed a new flag in 1964 and the achievements of Centennial Year. Sometimes, Canadian nationalism could be anti-American. International unions were an easy target. Canadian members grumbled that their union dues were spent in the United States and that strikes could be approved only by the American headquarters. In some unions, Canadian locals were forbidden to contribute to parties like the NDP.

Unions in Canada also had to face the growth of nationalism in Quebec. The movement for Quebec independence started early both among unions in the CNTU and among the Quebec locals of national and international unions affiliated to the Canadian Labour Congress. There were many grievances. Some unions were slow to serve their members in French. Contracts were printed in English to suit company management and union headquarters, though members sometimes only understood French. Many union leaders in Quebec were quick to identify with the independence movement that grew out of the Quiet

Revolution of the 1960s. At times, their strikes in the 1970s were directed as much against the Liberal government of Robert Bourassa as against public or private employers. Organized labour in Quebec played a prominent part in the victory of René Lévesque's Parti Québécois in 1976.

For most Canadians, even in Quebec, inflation and unemployment were just as important as nationalism. The 1960s had brought many benefits for ordinary people. The Canada Pension Plan introduced in 1966 was a start on a social security system that did not depend on holding a single job for most of one's life. In 1967, union members shared the credit for introducing a health insurance program for all Canadians. In most provinces, systems of student loans and grants helped young people to go to university or community college. Canadians welcomed these policies in the 1960s, but they had to pay for them in the 1970s.

As the decade advanced, it was harder to see that Canada was making headway. Economic experts had often said that a country might have either high unemployment or rapidly rising prices. Now Canada, and many other countries, suffered from both evils at once. People could blame the Arabs for their oil monopoly. They could complain about the government, the corporations or the unions. Since unions made a lot of noise with their wage demands, they made a good target.

Changes to labour legislation in the 1970s generally made it easier for workers to form unions. A new Canada Labour Code gave many employees the right to discuss technological changes before they were adopted. Union members gained new laws to protect health and safety at work. But the real debate in the 1970s was over inflation.

Businessmen insisted that they had to meet rising costs. Union leaders argued that their members only negotiated contracts after months and even years of watching their wages shrink. Some people claimed that the problem could only be solved by government controls on both wages and prices. At first, Mr. Trudeau sneered at the idea but, on Thanksgiving week-end, 1975, he announced strict wage and price restraint, enforced by a new Anti-Inflation Board.

At first, many Canadians welcomed the news. People who had seen wages and pensions shrink with inflation hoped for rescue. Most unions, however, fought the new program. Their members found prices rising while their wages were held down. The Canadian Labour Congress organized protest rallies, challenges in the courts and a na-

Workers protest the federal government's wage and price restraints in 1976. While many Canadians welcomed government action, union members complained that their wages were controlled while prices continued to rise.

tional "Day of Protest" on October 15, 1976. By early 1978, the program ended.

Perhaps people will never agree about the success of Canada's anti-inflation program. Supporters argue that inflation fell from eleven to eight percent in three years. Others insist that the rate would have fallen anyway and that controls caused many of the lay-offs and shut-downs that followed. When unions were free to ask for higher wages, they had to do so at a time when more Canadians were out of work than at any time since the Great Depression. Union leaders, caught between their members' frustration and hardening company resistance, found themselves in a difficult position.

One possible outlet was renewed political action. Under an aggressive new president, Dennis McDermott, the CLC decided to help its neglected partner, the New Democratic Party. The first results were disappointing. NDP gains in the 1979 and 1980 elections were small and seemed to bear little connection with the union effort. What the CLC had learned was that union members and their families needed convincing that the NDP really was "their" party.

Another problem for the Canadian Labour Congress in the 1980s was the loss of some of its oldest affiliates. A new Quebec law designed to end bitter union battles on construction sites allowed only one organization per site. The CLC's Quebec Federation of Labour started its own construction union. The international construction unions were furious. They also disliked the way rank-and-file delegates dominated the Canadian Labour Congress conventions. In contrast, the AFL-CIO had a system of hand-picked union representatives. By 1981, twelve of the CLC's construction union affiliates had left to form their own central organization.

Into the Future

Canadian working people and their unions entered the 1980s in a gloomy mood. In the United States, unions had shrunk to represent only about one American worker in five. Canadian unions were much stronger but they were also under attack.

In the century and a half that unions have been their major weapon, working people in Canada have made great progress. Men and women have won the vote. Poverty is now the grim fate of a minority, not a majority. Most people have been freed from the fear of huge hospital and medical bills. Workers no longer face unemployment with the likelihood that they will be unable to feed themselves or their families. Workers injured on the job have a right to compensation. Health and safety laws make sure that fewer workers lose their lives or their well-being on the job.

In 1886, a leading Toronto newspaper declared that labour unions had outlived their usefulness. Once, the paper admitted, unions had been necessary because employers were unfair and workers were badly treated. But by 1886, it maintained, that was no longer true. Unions had become too powerful and greedy. Their members were too willing to make the public suffer through strikes.

A hundred years from now, will people read the similar comments in our newspapers and smile? Through unions, working people have helped to make Canada a good place to live. Chances are, if they keep trying, it can be better yet.

Selected Biographies

DRAPER, Patrick M. (1868-1943)

When Paddy Draper became secretary-treasurer of the Trades and Labour Congress in 1900, he had to open an office in his own home. When he retired in 1939, he was president of the largest labour organization in Canada, with a membership of a quarter million. A compositor by trade, he became director of printing at the Government Printing Bureau in Ottawa. A shrewd, cautious man, Draper was a trusted adviser on trade union affairs for prime ministers from Sir Robert Borden to William Lyon Mackenzie King.

HARTMAN, Grace (1919-   )

Born in Toronto, Grace Hartman worked as a secretary for the Borough of North York. By 1959, she was president of her local union, and when the Canadian Union of Public Employees was formed in 1963, she was elected a regional vice-president for Ontario. She was an outspoken leader in the fight for collective bargaining rights for municipal and schoolboard employees. In 1967 she was elected national secretary-treasurer of CUPE, and in 1975, when it had become Canada's largest labour organization, Grace Hartman became the first woman to lead a Canadian Union.

JODOIN, Claude (1913-1975)

Claude Jodoin would have studied to become a surgeon if the Depression had not wiped out his family's fortune. Instead, he went to work. By 1937, he was an organizer for the International Ladies' Garment Workers' Union. In Montreal, he became a powerful and respected union leader, elected to the city council and to the Quebec legislature. In 1954, Claude Jodoin was elected president of the Trades and Labour Congress in time to lead it into the merger that created the Canadian Labour Congress. As first president of the CLC, he helped create the New Democratic Party. He also made the CLC a strong voice in international labour organizations.

KING, William Lyon Mackenzie (1874-1950)

A grandson of William Lyon Mackenzie, the Upper Canadian rebel, King was educated at the University of Toronto and Harvard. In 1900, he was appointed as Canada's first deputy minister of labour. His success in settling disputes helped take him into Sir Wilfrid Laurier's government as Minister of Labour in 1908. King's philosophy of industrial relations won him world-wide recognition and a career with the Rockefeller interests, but in 1919 he returned to Canada to become leader of the Liberal party. With two interruptions, King was prime minister of Canada from 1921 until 1948. He often applied his approach to labour mediation to Canadian political problems and always took a direct interest in labour issues.

McLACHLAN, James B. (1870-1936)

Born and bred in Scotland, Jimmy McLachlan was working as a miner before he was in his teens. He came to Canada in 1900 and was the leader of Nova Scotia's coal miners during the bitter strikes of 1909 and the 1920s. A passionate speaker and writer, McLachlan is still remembered, even by those who disagreed with him, as one of the greatest leaders of Canadian labour. A life-long crusader and radical, he died in poverty, commemorated by such phrases as: ". . . under capitalism, the working class has but two courses to follow: crawl or fight."

MILLARD, Charles H. (1896-1980)

Charles Millard was born in St. Thomas, Ontario, and trained as a carpenter. After his small woodworking business went under during the Depression, he went to work at General Motors in Oshawa and led the first Canadian local of the United Autoworkers in the 1937 strike. In 1942, Millard became Canadian director of the United Steelworkers. When he resigned in 1956 to devote himself to union organizing in the Third World, the Steelworkers had become the biggest union in Canada. Millard, who had been an early supporter of the CCF, was an architect of the New Democratic Party and a life-long crusader against the Communists.

MOSHER, Aaron R. (1881-1959)

A fifth-generation Canadian of Dutch ancestry, Aaron Mosher was born near Halifax. He left school at the age of fifteen and went to work as a miner, a clerk and a freight handler. In 1907, he led a successful strike for better working conditions and, in 1908, became the first president of a new Canadian Brotherhood of Railway Employees. It soon became the largest transportation union in Canada. In the 1920s, Mosher became a foe of international unions, but in 1940, when national and CIO unions joined in the Canadian Congress of Labour, he became the first and only president. Mosher was a forceful person, a strong chairman for the CCL's turbulent meetings and a reformer with an open, inquiring mind.

O'DONOGHUE, Daniel (1844-1907)

An Irish-born printer, Dan O'Donoghue came to Canada in 1852. He was apprenticed in Ottawa, worked in the United States and returned to the Canadian capital to play a leading role in the local unions. In 1874, he was the first labour man ever elected to the Ontario legislature. An early advocate of accident prevention, workmen's compensation laws and technical education, O'Donoghue was an active organizer for the Knights of Labour and a leading figure in the early Trades and Labour Congress. When he died, he was widely known as the "Father of Canadian Labour."

WOODSWORTH, James Shaver (1874-1942)

A Methodist minister whose father had established missions across the West, J. S. Woodsworth worked among the immigrants and poor people of north-end Winnipeg. That experience and his pacifism cut him off from his church and led him to support trade unionism and democratic socialism. Elected to Parliament in 1921 as a Labour MP, he maintained his independence, formed a small group and showed that a third party could gain valuable concessions such as Canada's first old age pension legislation. In 1932, Woodsworth led in the formation of the Co-operative Commonwealth Federation. He hoped that it would be only the first step in creating a strong labour party in Canada.

Glossary

Agreement, collective   A contract between one or more unions and one or more employers covering wages, hours, working conditions, benefits and procedures for settling disputes and grievances.

Arbitration   A way of settling disputes through a third party, either a single *arbitrator* or a board made up of a chairperson and one or more representatives for each side. Arbitration may be voluntary or compulsory. The decision of the arbitrator or board is final and both sides are obliged to accept it.

Bargaining unit   A group of workers in a craft, plant, industry or occupation considered suitable for representation by a union for purposes of collective bargaining.

Checkoff   An agreement authorizing an employer to deduct union dues, and sometimes other amounts, from a worker's wages. These amounts are forwarded to the union.

Closed Shop   A requirement in a collective agreement that the employer hire only workers who are union members in good standing and that new employees be hired through the union.

Collective bargaining   Way of establishing wages, hours and other conditions of employment by negotiations between the union and the employer. Usually collective bargaining results in a written contract which covers all employees in the bargaining unit whether they are union members or not.

Company Union   A union entirely made up of the employees of one company and often organized and dominated by the employer.

Conciliation   A way of settling a labour dispute by compromise. It differs from arbitration in that the parties are not obliged to accept the proposal of the conciliator or board. Also described as *mediation*.

Contract   *See* Agreement, collective

Craft union   A trade union which usually limits membership to a specific skill or craft, for example electricians or plumbers.

Fringe benefit   A non-wage benefit such as paid vacations, pensions, life insurance, the cost of which is borne in whole or in part by the employer.

Grievance   A complaint by one or more employees or a union claiming a breach of the collective agreement or an injustice.

Industrial union   A union based on organizing all the workers in an industry regardless of craft or skill.

International union   A union with members in both Canada and the United States.

Local   The basic unit of union organization. Each local has its own constitution, elected members and responsibility for bargaining and administering its contract.

Lockout   The closing of a workplace by an employer to bring pressure on workers to settle a labour dispute on terms favourable to the employer.

Mediation   *See* Conciliation

Moonlighting   Holding by an individual of more than one paid job at a time.

National union   A union whose membership is limited to Canada.

Pickets   Union members stationed outside a place of work or business to publicize the existence of a labour dispute and discourage other workers or customers from entering.

Rand Formula   A clause in a collective agreement in which employers agree to deduct an amount equal to union dues from all members of the bargaining unit, whether or not they belong to the union.

Seniority   An employee's status according solely or mainly to length of service.

Shop steward   A union official, usually a member of the work force, who represents the union and its members in grievances and other union business.

Strike   A work stoppage to pressure an employer into agreeing to terms or conditions of employment. A strike is normally legal only when a collective agreement is not in force. "Wildcat strikes" break the collective agreement and are not authorized by the union.

Strikebreaker   A person who continues to work during a strike or takes a job to replace workers on strike. Sometimes called a "scab."

Union label   A tag, label or imprint on a product showing that it was produced by union members. Also called the "bug."

Union Shop   A requirement in a collective agreement that every worker covered by the agreement become and remain a union member. New workers who are not union members may be hired on condition that they join the union within a specified time.

Work-to-rule   A form of slowdown in which workers obey all the laws and rules applying to their work.

For Discussion

CHAPTER 1

1) Define the following words: craftsmen, union, inflation, strike, negotiate, dues, contract, mediator, lockout, grievance, union label, picket.
2) Explain briefly: collective bargaining, international union, policy convention, industrial union, craft union, adversary system.
3) Keep a list of the labour organizations mentioned in this chapter. Beside the name write a brief explanation.
4) If you had attended the meeting of Local 357, would you have supported a strike? Write the speech you might have made outlining your views.
5) Why do union members try to support each other, even when they are not directly affected? Is this a good idea?
6) When students have a *grievance*, would it be a good idea to have the support of a student union? Would there be any bad features of this?
7) Organize a debate on the topic: Resolved: Unions are (not) Necessary.
8) Rewrite the Local 357 illustration as a short play which will help students understand how unions work. Feel free to change the dialogue and characters.
9) Start collecting news clippings relating to the labour movement. Do any of these clippings reveal pro- or anti-union bias?

CHAPTER 2

1) Define these terms: poorhouse, tariff, unskilled labourer, fraternal order.
2) Draw a line down a sheet of notepaper. On the line locate each of the unions mentioned in this chapter in the order of their appearance.
3) How did Macdonald's National Policy affect the labour movement?
4) Why were each of these people important to the labour movement: Daniel O'Donoghue, George Brown, John A. Macdonald?
5) A hundred years ago Canadian working people lived very different lives. What kind of wages and hours of work were common? Why did women and children earn so much less than men?
6) Imagine you are an employer in 1850. Write a speech telling your employees why they should not join a union.
7) Imagine you are a worker in 1850. Write a speech to your fellow workers explaining why they should form a union.

CHAPTER 3

1) Define these words: compensation, wobbly, navvies, capitalist.
2) Draw a line diagram on which are located the unions and labour organizations mentioned in this chapter. Write one sentence describing each.
3) Using one sentence for each, explain how the following people were important to the labour movement: Paddy Draper, John Flett, James Lougheed, James Dunsmuir, Mackenzie King, Sir Joseph Flavelle, Bob Russell.
4) What was the Industrial Disputes Investigation Act?

5) Why did so many workers join the Knights of Labour in the 1880s? Why did the Knights collapse so quickly?
6) What were Sam Gompers's three principles for successful union organization? Why were they so important? How did these principles limit union strength?
7) How was the Winnipeg General Strike (1919) different from other strikes? Why did it happen? Was it really an attempted revolution?
8) Write a short play based on the logging accident described in this chapter.

CHAPTER 4

1) Write a definition for the following words: statistics, credit, reformer, company, socialism, conscription, Bolsheviks, Prohibition.
2) Identify these people: J. S. Woodsworth, R. B. Bennett, Aaron Mosher, Tim Buck, Karl Marx, Franklin Roosevelt, John L. Lewis, Charles Millard.
3) What was achieved by organized labour in the 1920s?
4) What did 1929 statistics reveal about the Canadian standard of living?
5) In the 1920s, Canadian unions split into warring camps. List four of the major labour organizations in Canada by 1930. Why did the split occur?
6) Why did many Canadian unions support the CIO so fervently in the 1930s?
7) Why was it difficult for a farmer/labour party to work?
8) Union members are often disturbed because any use of the strike weapon is given wide publicity whereas the many peaceful collective agreements are hardly mentioned in the press. How could this be resolved?

CHAPTER 5

1) How did these people view the labour movement: C. D. Howe, C. P. McTague, M. L. Coldwell, Maurice Duplessis, Jean Marchand, Joey Smallwood?
2) What role did the Communists play in the labour movement in Canada?
3) Why did so many strikes occur in 1946? What were the results?
4) What is P.C. 1003 and why was it so important?
5) Why was life so much better for most Canadians after the Second World War than it had been after the First World War?
6) Why did the Canadian Labour Congress decide to help start its own political party? Was this a good idea?
8) 'Scab' is one of the powerful negative words in our vocabulary. Why?

CHAPTER 6

1) Define the following words: automation, wildcat strike, civil servant.
2) Why did unions grow in the 1960s?
3) Why did many Canadians attack the international unions?
4) In some European countries, workers elect directors to help manage their own companies. Would this be a good idea in Canada? What are the problems for the workers and for the company?
5) By law, employees of private companies can form a union and go on strike. Should public employees have the same right? Should teachers, policemen or tax collectors have the right to strike? If not, how can their interests be protected?
6) Are unions responsible for rising prices and unemployment?
7) Do you agree with the principle of free collective bargaining?

Index